The Essential
POLICE CONSTABLE DEGREE APPRENTICESHIP

EPA HANDBOOK

Other policing titles from Critical Publishing

The Professional Policing Curriculum in Practice
Series edited by Tony Blockley

Criminal Investigation
Iain Stainton and Robert Ewin   ISBN: 978-1-914171-50-5

Police Research and Evidence-based Policing
Emma Spooner, Craig Hughes and Phil Mike Jones   ISBN: 978-1-914171-86-4

Police Procedure and Evidence in the Criminal Justice System
Barrie Archer and George Ellison   ISBN: 978-1-914171-98-7

Understanding Policing and Professional Practice
Barrie Sheldon and Peter Williams   ISBN: 978-1-914171-95-6

Critical Study Skills: Policing

Academic Writing and Referencing for your Policing Degree
Jane Bottomley, Steven Pryjmachuk and Martin Wright   ISBN: 978-1-913063-41-2

Communication Skills for your Policing Degree
Jane Bottomley, Steven Pryjmachuk and Martin Wright   ISBN: 978-1-913063-49-8

Critical Thinking Skills for your Policing Degree
Jane Bottomley, Steven Pryjmachuk and Martin Wright   ISBN: 978-1-913063-45-0

Studying for your Policing Degree
Jane Bottomley, Steven Pryjmachuk and Martin Wright   ISBN: 978-1-913063-17-7

The Essential
POLICE CONSTABLE DEGREE APPRENTICESHIP

EPA HANDBOOK

SHARON GANDER

First published in 2023 by Critical Publishing Ltd

All rights reserved. No part of this publication may be reproduced, stored in a retrieval system, or transmitted in any form or by any means, electronic, mechanical, photocopying, recording or otherwise, without prior permission in writing from the publisher.

The author has made every effort to ensure the accuracy of information contained in this publication, but assumes no responsibility for any errors, inaccuracies, inconsistencies and omissions. Likewise, every effort has been made to contact copyright holders. If any copyright material has been reproduced unwittingly and without permission the Publisher will gladly receive information enabling them to rectify any error or omission in subsequent editions.

Copyright © 2023 Sharon Gander

British Library Cataloguing in Publication Data
A CIP record for this book is available from the British Library

ISBN: 978-1-915080-71-4

This book is also available in the following e-book formats:
EPUB ISBN: 978-1-915080-72-1
Adobe e-book ISBN: 978-1-915080-73-8

The right of Sharon Gander to be identified as the Author of this work has been asserted by her in accordance with the Copyright, Design and Patents Act 1988.

Text design by Greensplash
Cover design by Out of House Limited
Project management by Newgen Publishing UK
Printed and bound in Great Britain by 4edge, Essex

Critical Publishing
3 Connaught Road
St Albans
AL3 5RX

www.criticalpublishing.com

Printed on FSC accredited paper

Dedication

This book is dedicated to my amazing Mom, Dad, Callum and my sunbeam Maisie x

To order our books please go to our website www.criticalpublishing.com or contact our distributor Ingram Publisher Services, telephone 01752 202301 or email IPSUK. orders@ingramcontent.com. Details of bulk order discounts can be found at www. criticalpublishing.com/delivery-information.

Our titles are also available in electronic format: for individual use via our website and for libraries and other institutions from all the major ebook platforms.

Contents

About the author viii

Acknowledgements ix

Foreword x

1 Introduction to the Police Constable Degree Apprenticeship 1
2 Your PCDA programme journey 12
3 The PCDA support triangle 29
4 Getting prepared for your EPA gateway 48
5 Understanding, planning and preparing for your assessments 66
6 EPA day: pass first time 81
7 Programme and EPA overview and checklist 106

References 113

Appendix 1: Mapping of the Police Constable Apprenticeship Standards to the EPA (KSBs) 116

Appendix 2: Professional discussion: assessment criteria underpinning KSBs/operational competence 121

Index 126

About the author

Sharon Gander has extensive experience in police education, including training new police officer recruits for West Midlands, West Mercia and Warwickshire Police. She is a senior lecturer in policing at Sheffield Hallam University and was previously a course leader for Police Constable Degree Apprenticeship (PCDA) programmes for West Midlands Police at Staffordshire University. Sharon is also an Independent EPA Assessor at Northumbria University, and sits as a board member of the Police Education Qualification Framework (PEQF) Initial Policing Education Board for the College of Policing.

Acknowledgements

I would like to express my heartfelt gratitude and appreciation to Julia and Lily at Critical Publishing for their help, guidance and support in writing this book. I am very fortunate to have had incredible support from my employers and colleagues at Sheffield Hallam University when writing this book, thank you.

Thank you to my lovely friend and colleague, Vicky Sparkes, for giving me permission to use your RAISE reflective model in my book.

A massive thank you to my PhD supervisors at Staffordshire University, Dr Laura Walton-Williams and Dr Lauren Metcalfe, for your patience while I disappeared for a few months to write this book, researching my area of interest – the Police Constable Degree Apprenticeship (PCDA) EPA.

Finally, a big shoutout to all the incredible PCDA student officers who work and study tirelessly to make the world a better place. You are the future of policing and you all rock! I am very humbled and grateful to be part of your learner journey (albeit a tiny part) and wish you all every success in your police career. I wrote this book for you to guide you through the programme and achieve the top grades that you aspire to achieve; I hope it assists you.

Foreword

If you consider any professional career path, you will find opportunities for accredited learning and the chance to have your dedication and expertise in a given field rewarded with a recognised qualification. Policing has been one of the few exceptions to this, and generations of officers giving decades of service in highly skilled fields gained no formal qualifications during their service. This incongruity has now rightly been remedied with the introduction of the new police education pathways and the Police Constable Degree Apprenticeship (PCDA).

The end-point assessment (EPA) is the culmination of a student officer's efforts over the three-year PCDA programme. Those of us with a long career in policing behind us will still remember our initial training when we joined the police. The new pathways represent a significant change to how police education and training is delivered and it is welcomed that student officers will now achieve a recognised degree-level qualification at the end of their training programme.

Sharon has been involved in the development and implementation of the Police Education Qualification Framework (PEQF) pathways nationally and EPA from the onset. She brings a unique experience base to the area of police education having been a police officer, police trainer and now a senior lecturer in policing at Sheffield Hallam University. Sharon is also an Independent Assessor for the EPA so is certainly qualified to give a clear insight into the requirements to successfully navigate the EPA.

The most important person in all of this is, of course, the student officer. The EPA can be a daunting hurdle for them; both universities and employers have a clear moral duty to prepare and support them for this challenge. This book will be invaluable to all involved in the EPA process, including employers, work-based coaches and university staff, to support, guide and help student officers to pass the assessment process. This book will be invaluable to the student officer in removing the fog that surrounds any new process and giving them clear practical guidance as to how to prepare and pass first time. The information in this book is grounded and drawn from actual experience of assessing the EPA and draws upon the early lessons learned by student officers who have already been through this process.

Steve Ashman
Former Chief Constable, Northumbria Police

1 Introduction to the Police Constable Degree Apprenticeship

> **LEARNING OBJECTIVES**
>
> After reading this chapter you will be able to:
>
> - identify the key components of *Policing Vision 2025* and the requirement to transform policing recruitment and education;
> - understand the Policing Education and Qualifications Framework;
> - explain the benefits of the Police Constable Degree Apprenticeship.

Introduction

Congratulations. You are either about to embark on your journey to become a police officer or are already on a programme and preparing for your final assessment. *The Essential Police Constable Degree Apprenticeship EPA Handbook* has been written to support and guide you through the Police Constable Degree Apprenticeship (PCDA) and ensure that you are fully prepared to undertake your final assessment – the end-point assessment (EPA) – at the end of Year 3. This will be the final component of your policing apprenticeship before you are signed off as a fully competent police officer.

This book guides you through the basics of the PCDA programme, ensuring that you are preparing for your final assessment from day one of your university programme and employment with the police. It is intended to ensure you successfully pass the EPA on your first attempt. Planning and preparation are key, and this book provides you with essential information and top tips to incorporate into both your study and work life throughout the course.

This book also supports university and police staff who teach/support the PCDA programme. It enables staff to be fully equipped to support and guide their students through the process. As the PCDA is a newly implemented programme of study for new-recruit police officers, there is currently a lack of substantive guidance for staff and students on the PCDA programme. The information contained in this book therefore supports and guides all involved in the process.

The book is structured around specific elements of the PCDA programme to ensure that you are fully prepared and ready to pass your EPA. It details changes to how police officers are recruited and trained and the key information you need regarding your programme of study. It is recommended that the first time that you read this book, start from the very beginning and work your way through to the end in order. This will ensure that you have a clear understanding of the process and are knowledgeable about the key information regarding the PCDA and EPA. As you progress through your police apprenticeship, you can go to relevant chapters as and when required.

Skills and knowledge requirements of the PCDA

This book equips you with the required skills and knowledge to pass the PCDA EPA with flying colours. The EPA is an opportunity for you to demonstrate to your Independent Assessor the skills and knowledge you have gained on your learning journey as a student police officer during your policing apprenticeship. This handbook ensures that you are fully prepared, confident and organised for your final assessment.

TASK

Key tip – 'By failing to prepare, you are preparing to fail.'

- Do you know to whom this quote is attributed?
- What is meant by this statement?

Structure of this book

This handbook is written in chronological order to match your experiences as you progress through your policing apprenticeship. There are case study examples in many of the chapters which give you an overview of experiences from some student officers who have completed their EPA. There are also tasks throughout the book for you to self-reflect on your progress throughout your PCDA journey. The PCDA is a bespoke learning experience for each student officer and there is a wealth of support and guidance to assist you to pass the EPA on your first attempt. Each chapter gives you top tips to support you throughout your PCDA programme. As each university and police collaboration is bespoke, always check your online learning platform for current advice regarding assignment submissions and EPA structure. The delivery methods may vary nationally but the EPA assessment criteria will be standard for each training provider and police force.

Chapter 1: Introduction to the Police Constable Degree Apprenticeship

This chapter details the recent changes introduced to the recruitment and training of police officers in the service after the publication of *Policing Vision 2025*. It covers the new recruitment pathways and the PCDA. It details the new collaborative approach to police education and the learner-focused approach which involves the employer, training provider and apprentice. The chapter also details the positive aspects of work-based learning where you will put your knowledge and skills learnt at university into practice when you undertake your operational placements with the police (HM Government, 2022a).

Chapter 2: Your PCDA programme journey

This chapter introduces you to the three-year PCDA programme, its components and what to expect during your learning journey. It details the importance of time management and effective planning both at university and when on duty with the police. The key contacts in the police and at university who support and guide you through your apprenticeship are also detailed. This chapter also covers the different ways that you will be assessed during your PCDA programme, and the importance of successfully completing all key milestones to progress to the next level of your programme.

Chapter 3: The PCDA support triangle

This chapter introduces you to the importance of working closely with your employer, the police and with university staff, who deliver the academic aspect of your apprenticeship programme. This chapter also details the importance of attending regular tripartite reviews to ensure you are on track to complete the PCDA. Regular attendance at tripartite meetings will ensure that you have support and guidance throughout your PCDA programme. Specific support and guidance are discussed in this chapter if you have additional learning needs in the classroom and in the workplace, such as dyslexia. The importance of critical self-reflection with regard to operational policing and academic study is also covered in this chapter.

Chapter 4: Getting prepared for your EPA gateway

In this chapter, you are introduced to the concept of the gateway requirement of the EPA. When you have successfully completed the required knowledge and skills, you will move through the gateway and be ready to undertake your EPA. This chapter covers the importance of being prepared for the EPA and includes the key definitions and information required so you pass through the gateway with ease. Also detailed in this chapter is the requirement to review the evidence-based research project assessment criteria and produce a plan to achieve these requirements.

Chapter 5: Understanding, planning and preparing for your assessments

This chapter considers good practice when preparing for assessments throughout your PCDA programme and finally the EPA. There are examples of assessments you will undergo throughout your programme, preparing you for what may be included in your final EPA. This chapter also covers the importance of the mock session before your final EPA to ensure that you are fully prepared for your final assessment. The key people involved in your learner journey and EPA are detailed in this chapter.

Chapter 6: EPA day: pass first time

This chapter covers in detail the requirements to successfully navigate and pass your EPA first time. You are given top tips, suggestions and information regarding what the EPA Independent Assessors are looking for when grading your EPA. There is a clear outline of what preparation must be completed before your EPA day. Guidance will be given on how to achieve the highest grade attainable for the EPA – a distinction. This chapter includes real student case studies and scenarios to assist you and consolidate the information in this chapter.

Chapter 7: Programme and EPA overview and checklist

This chapter details the importance of planning for key milestones and your EPA from the start of your PCDA programme. The importance of critical self-reflection throughout your apprenticeship and how reflection can improve your professional practice when on duty with the police and in the classroom are covered in this chapter. There are detailed checklists in this chapter that list the key milestones which must be achieved to progress to the next level of your PCDA programme.

Recent changes to police recruitment pathways and education of new recruits

In 2016, the National Police Chiefs' Council (NPCC) published *Policing Vision 2025*, which set out a plan for policing over the next decade. Its main aim was to shape decisions around the transformation of all police services. The main consideration was how police services used their resources to keep people safe, in an effective and accessible way that could be trusted by the people they serve. The NPCC recognised that communities that the police serve were increasingly diverse and complex. This necessitated a more sophisticated response to the challenges that the police service were facing at the time of writing, and in the future. There has been a significant change in crime committed over recent years which the police have to deal with. Crimes such as child sexual exploitation, domestic abuse, cybercrime or new threats from serious and organised crime such as human trafficking needed to be dealt with differently due to their complex nature. The leaders of the police service – police and crime commissioners and chief constables – acknowledged that if they were to meet the future needs of communities, the service must continue to adapt to the modern police environment (NPCC, 2016).

Policing Vision 2025 was more than making savings or incremental reform of the police service; the ambition was to make transformative changes across the police service. One of the substantive recommendations was a significant change to how the police service recruited and trained their new-recruit police officers. It was imperative that the police service would attract and retain a workforce of confident professionals able to operate with a high degree of autonomy and accountability. This would ensure that the link between communities and the police would continue to form the bedrock of British policing. Change was needed to be better prepared to respond to existing and emerging crime types such as digital crime. They recognised that when the nature of crime changes, so must the skills of the workforce. Because of these recommendations, there has been a significant change made to the national policing curriculum by the College of Policing. The new police curriculum has incorporated higher-level thinking and analysis to empower new police officers to make decisions when on duty in quick time. This would mean that forces will be better at tackling crime and that the public would have greater confidence in the police.

The NPCC realised that the only way to address the new policing challenges without reducing the quality of services was to completely transform their approach to policing. During consultation, it was apparent that most forces did not have a thorough evidence-based understanding of police demands. This made it very difficult to transform services intelligently and to demonstrate they are achieving value for money. It was recommended to fill the gap by working with a range of partner agencies such as universities, using the expertise of academics in the training of new police recruits.

Important key recommendations for police recruitment and training

- Setting clear routes to enter, leave and re-enter policing that are clear, flexible and consistently applied across the service.
- Setting clear and consistent requirements for entry into policing and for accreditation into defined ranks.
- Supporting key aspects of police training and development through academic accreditation which recognises the skills and knowledge of the workforce.
- Supporting the workforce through change so that they feel valued and retain their commitment and sense of vocation to meet the new challenges (NPCC, 2016).

The Policing Education Qualifications Framework

The Policing Education Qualifications Framework (PEQF) is a professional training framework for police officers and staff. It is based on a modern curriculum of dynamic operational training underpinned by sound theoretical education. The PEQF is currently focused on new joiners, but will be developed to cover a range of professional training in the future.

As previously mentioned, *Policing Vision 2025* highlighted the need for consistency, accreditation and defined roles. It identified different roles within the police service that required specific skills and knowledge. This would be backed by qualifications for different ranks in the police service. Until the PEQF was introduced, when police officers left the service there was no recognition of the training courses attended and skills and knowledge obtained during their role. The introduction of the PEQF will certainly address this issue over time.

Before the introduction of the new PEQF frameworks, the traditional entry route and police training given was under the Initial Police Learning and Development Programme (IPLDP). There were many issues with this route and training as police forces recruited differently without standard entry requirements, learning provision and support. The IPLDP was a largely classroom-based training programme, with little opportunity to put newly learned knowledge and skills into practice for many months at a time. The new PEQF programmes address this shortfall. The service recognised the need to standardise these areas as a priority due to the pressure on the service currently to adhere to strict recruitment targets under the commitment to recruit 20,000 officers by 2023. The IPLDP programme will operate in a small number of forces such as the Metropolitan Police until phased out in April 2023.

In July 2019, Boris Johnson announced a national campaign (dubbed the 'Boris uplift') to recruit 20,000 new police officers by March 2023 (Home Office, 2019). The police recruitment drive was the biggest in decades after significant cuts to police numbers since 2010. This coincided with the change in police recruitment and police education with aspirations of widening the gateway to and broadening the appeal of joining the service.

The College of Policing (2020) stated that there is increasing demand on the police to do more than just solve crime and 'catch the bad guys'. An important consideration of the introduction of the PEQF in the police service is that it recognised the level of expertise of police officers and valued their contribution and will be offering programmes of study to officers in higher ranks in the future.

TASK

- Why is it important that student officers have the opportunity to put knowledge and theory learnt in the classroom into practice when on operational work placements with the police?

- What is your preferred learning style (for example, are you more of a visual learner)?

- What might you be able to do to strengthen the way you learn using other methods?

Aims of the PEQF

- To provide a consistent and standardised high standard of training for all police officers whichever way they choose to join the force.
- To address the long-held deficiency in recognising the level at which police officers operate.
- To provide a framework with the College of Policing so they can revise the learning provision for all officers and staff. This will start with the initial entry routes to ensure they meet the needs of forces and the expectations of the service set out in *Policing Vision 2025*.
- To standardise the learning provision across all forces, in particular the initial learning for newly recruited officers.
- To include processes and guidance to help existing officers and staff achieve their potential. This will include taking their prior experience and learning achievement of transferable skills into consideration when wanting to study higher qualifications.
- Recognition of Prior Experience and Learning (RPL) to be introduced that could potentially give serving/retired police officers and staff academic credits for their previous experience. This would include courses or learning programmes they may have completed during their service (College of Policing, 2020a).

PEQF programmes

The Police Constable Degree Apprenticeship (PCDA)

- It is a minimum three-year programme of study.
- Funded primarily through the Apprenticeship Levy.
- Delivered by a police force in collaboration with a higher education institution (HEI) or other training provider (with taught degree awarding powers).

Apprenticeship Levy

The Apprenticeship Levy was initiated by the UK government in April 2017 for all employers paying a wage bill of more than £3 million a year.

Employers such as police forces that meet this criterion are required to pay 0.5 per cent of their payroll each month as a levy tax. This levy can then be used and reinvested back into their workforce in the form of apprenticeship training (HMRC, 2016).

The benefits of policing apprenticeships

- Offers the opportunity to aspiring officers who do not hold a degree qualification to join the police service.

- You study for a professional policing degree which is funded by the police so there is no requirement to pay back student loans after you have finished your degree programme.
- Learn the skills and knowledge required for your role as a police officer in protected learning blocks at university. Then put this knowledge into practice when you are on duty with the police. Learning 'on the job' is a great way to build confidence in dealing with the public, dealing with crime and victims. You will gain hands-on experience throughout your apprenticeship in different areas with the police.
- You get paid to learn and have paid holiday leave.
- You will have 20 per cent 'off-the-job learning' factored in to your working hours to study at university to learn the skills and knowledge required for your role.
- Enjoy support, guidance and student discounts as a university student.
- Be assessed throughout your programme and at the end of your apprenticeship.
- Be on a career path with lots of potential and opportunities within the police service.
- Experience work placements in many areas of policing such as response and investigation.
- Have the opportunity to specialise in a particular area of policing in Year 3 and after you have successfully completed your probation and apprenticeship.

To apply for the PCDA

Individuals need two A levels or an equivalent level 3 qualification, as defined in the Educations and Skills Act 2008.

Key aspects of the PCDA programme

The PCDA is subject to policies and guidelines by the Institute for Apprenticeships and Technical Education and the Skills Funding Agency (England) and Estyn (Wales). These include the following.

- A requirement to achieve level 2 English and maths, before or during the programme (you are unable to successfully complete your apprenticeship until these qualifications are achieved). It is highly recommended that you are in possession of these qualifications before you start an apprenticeship due to work and study commitments, as they will be studied alongside your degree apprenticeship.
- Completion of an evidence-based research project (EBRP). The EBRP forms part of the final summative assessment, the EPA. These projects should be rooted

and aligned to force business needs – for example, in key priority areas such as domestic violence. This allows the student officer to research and offer new recommendations and investigate specific problems their force is experiencing.
- The project outcomes, once assessed and deemed to be of sufficiently high quality, can be shared via the College of Policing academic support unit and What Works Centre (College of Policing, 2022a). This enables other forces to benefit from and build on your research – an exciting prospect.

Degree Holder Entry Programme (DHEP)

- A two-year programme.
- It is fully funded by the police force.
- Gives the individual a Graduate Diploma in Professional Policing Practice (120 credits at level 6).
- Provides an opportunity to specialise in one of the core areas of policing such as response or investigation.

To apply for the DHEP programme

Individuals need a level 6 degree in any subject other than a degree in professional policing licensed by the College of Policing.

Key aspects of the degree-holder programme

When considering this type of programme, applicants should be aware that:

- the programme follows the national policing curriculum, but some elements are removed, such as research and study skills, as these are generic to degree-level programmes;
- it is delivered and assessed academically at level 6 throughout the programme.

Professional Policing Degree (PPD)

- Usually a three-year degree programme, though some higher education institutions are now offering an accelerated two-year condensed degree programme.
- Fully funded by the student.
- Delivered by a higher education institution only.
- Encourages students to interact with local forces to enrich their learning experience by joining the special constabulary.
- Provides an opportunity to research and specialise in one of the core areas of policing.

To apply for the PPD

Individuals need to meet the standard UCAS entry requirements set out by the higher education institution offering the degree.

Key aspects of the PPD

When considering this type of programme, applicants should be aware of the following.

- The degree programme is based on the national policing curriculum. This is a knowledge-only programme with no operational practice unlike the other programmes, unless they join the special constabulary.
- Students will need to apply to join the police service as a separate activity after successful completion of their degree. This application process involves successful completion of an assessment centre, fitness testing and security vetting.
- Students being recruited into a force after the PPD completion will be required to complete a short 'transition' course covering specific areas that are not part of the degree. This ensures that they are safe and lawful before being deployed into an operational role.

Specialising in these programmes

Each of the above programmes can include a focus in one of the core areas of policing. This enables student officers to achieve accredited detective status alongside the standard programme outcomes.

For PCDA and DHEP programmes, individuals need to complete:

- the National Investigators' Exam (NIE), which requires additional focused study and revision;
- specific criteria relating to the Professionalising Investigation Programme (PIP) level 2 occupational competence.

For PPD students, individuals will need to achieve Independent Patrol Status (IPS) so will need to be in the role of a special constable, working operationally within a police force. When IPS is complete, they could be deployed to an investigation team and work towards the successful achievement of the national investigators' exam and PIP level 2 occupational competence during the remainder of their two-year probation (College of Policing, 2022b).

Conclusion

The NPCC recognised that transformative change was needed in all areas of the police service to ensure that it was fit for purpose in the changing face of demand and crime. *Policing Vision 2025* was published by the NPCC in 2016 and put forward recommendations to achieve its aim of transforming the police service. As the communities that the police service are becoming more diverse and complex, it requires a more sophisticated response to deal with these challenges. To ensure that the workforce is equipped to do so, there has been a substantive change in how the police recruit and train police officers. Following the recommendations, the College of Policing created and implemented nationally the new PEQF entry routes and national police curriculum.

TASK

- Visit the websites below and make notes from the information available to you. It is very important that you are familiar with the websites and documents as they are key to your policing apprenticeship.

Further reading

College of Policing – the professional body for the police service and operationally independent of the government. The College of Policing supports professional development, sets standards and shares knowledge and practice.

> www.college.police.uk/about

End Point Assessment Plan for Police Constable Integrated Degree Apprenticeship – this document details the EPA plan which you are assessed on in Year 3.

> www.instituteforapprenticeships.org/media/1440/police-constable-assessment-plan.pdf

Institute for Apprenticeships and Technical Education (IfATE) – their vision is for world-leading apprenticeships that equip people from all backgrounds for skilled occupations. The IfATE, working with employers, develop, approve, review and revise apprenticeships.

> www.instituteforapprenticeships.org/about

Police Constable (Integrated Degree) Standard – this document contains information regarding the knowledge, skills and behaviours (KSBs) that you must successfully demonstrate and achieve during your PCDA.

> www.instituteforapprenticeships.org/apprenticeship-standards/police-constable-integrated-degree-v1-0

2 Your PCDA programme journey

> **LEARNING OBJECTIVES**
>
> After reading this chapter you will be able to:
>
> - identify the key educational principles of the Policing Education Qualifications Framework;
> - understand the key components of your police apprenticeship programme;
> - discuss the different ways you will be assessed during your PCDA journey;
> - explain the importance of successfully completing all milestones to progress to the next academic year of your programme.

The Police Constable Degree Apprenticeship programme

The PCDA programme is three years in duration. It is an integrated degree apprenticeship, which means that a degree qualification is included in the apprenticeship programme. You will be assessed as you progress through the apprenticeship, with the final assessment to complete being the end-point assessment (EPA) (ESFA, 2022a). After successful completion of both your operational competencies and academic studies, you will be awarded a degree in Professional Police Practice. You will then successfully complete your probation as a student police officer and be confirmed in post as a substantive police officer.

The structure, content and academic progression of the national degree specification for the apprenticeship is founded upon the College of Policing national policing curriculum (College of Policing, 2020a). All indicative content in this degree specification must be included in your apprenticeship programme. Although the PCDA curriculum is standardised and the same nationwide, the actual programme that you are studying will be bespoke to your employing police force. When your police force and university were contracted to provide education programmes to new recruits, they set out a plan of the requirements of their force. The police force collaborated with the university to develop and deliver a programme bespoke to its specific needs and requirements. There are specific criteria that must be included in each year, as discussed later in this chapter, but other content will be distributed throughout the three-year programme.

The educational principles of the PEQF

The new police constable apprenticeship constitutes a core element of the Policing Education Qualifications Framework (PEQF). The PEQF has been developed in accordance with the following educational principles.

- **Meeting the professional requirements of twenty-first-century policing.** The PEQF supports the evolution of a more highly skilled, flexible workforce, capable of working more autonomously and efficiently. Police officers will need less supervision and will employ greater use of discretion. The curriculum is reviewed on an annual basis in order to anticipate and meet the current and emerging challenges of twenty-first-century policing. This underpins the provision of the best possible professional service by the police. It is very important during your degree programme that your curriculum is current, and you are taught the most up-to-date law, legislation and professional practice. This is also a great way to cascade new information to existing officers on your operational placements as you may be the first to be informed of the new developments and information at university.

- **Ensuring national consistency of professional education.** The College of Policing is committed to establishing and maintaining national consistency and standardisation in meeting the professional educational needs of the police force. This was one of the main issues of the Initial Police Learning and Development Programme (IPLDP) and why there was a need to change the old system of police education. Each force had different ways of delivering the training and the curriculum content could vary significantly from force to force. With the new PEQF, all forces have the same curriculum and if you want to transfer to a new force, you will not have to complete initial training again as the training is standardised nationally.

- **Championing a values-based, ethical approach to policing.** The values underpinning police education are based on the Competency and Values Framework (College of Policing, 2017). The PEQF curriculum places fundamental emphasis upon adopting an ethical approach to policing as set out in the *Code of Ethics* (College of Policing, 2014), and centred upon serving, supporting and protecting the public.

- **Supporting equality of educational opportunity within the policing profession.** The PEQF supports equality of opportunity for entrants to the police service and throughout the educational stages associated with their professional development and progression. All members of the police service who are performing the same role/function should have access to the same professional educational opportunities. The new PEQF pathways have opened up new supporting routes for applicants who may have never considered university before due to personal circumstances. The PCDA offers a university qualification that is funded by the police. The PEQF also offers the opportunity for existing officers in all ranks to have the opportunity to study and obtain meaningful qualifications.

- **Developing a high-quality, evidence-based education for the policing profession.** The PEQF programmes foster the highest standards of educational and professional development within policing. They enhance competence in the policing profession, based upon an evidence-based policing approach. This is a new concept in police education and is likely to have a large impact on how policing is delivered nationally. During your programme in Year 3, you will have the opportunity to research an area of operational policing. Your ideas could be implemented nationally and make a significant impact to the police service.

- **Promoting a collaborative approach to education within the police service.** All PEQF programmes are developed and delivered by means of a practical, professional collaboration. They bring together in educational partnerships the best of what a combination of academic learning and applied professional practice can provide. This collaborative approach between the police and higher education institutions has probably been the most difficult to implement as it is such a significant change to how police officers are educated. Before the introduction of the PEQF, all initial training was delivered 'in house' by the police and it was understandably difficult to then share the delivery with a university or private outside provider. Since the first roll-out of PEQF programmes in 2018, these collaborative working relationships have become stronger and are making a positive difference.

- **Enabling continuing professional development in policing roles.** Everyone involved in the policing profession, whether police officers, police staff or volunteers, will have appropriate opportunities for continuing professional development (CPD). This will increase job satisfaction and will improve performance and progression within the wider policing profession, supporting advancement along appropriate career pathways. It is very important that the new PEQF education routes and pathways are inclusive to all staff (new and existing) to encourage a sense of belonging and the opportunity to achieve new qualifications in their role with the police service.

National degree apprenticeship standard for the police constable

The national apprenticeship standard sets the occupational profile for the role of the police constable. The constable role, by its very nature, requires application of a high degree of professional knowledge and skills across a range of complex and challenging situations and contexts. Linked to this role is the demonstration of appropriate behaviours congruent with effective and appropriate front-line policing. This apprenticeship standard, which has been approved at level 6 by the Institute for Apprenticeships and Technical Education (IfATE, the government department with responsibility for apprenticeships), specifies in detail the knowledge, skills and behaviours required for the successful professional performance of this core policing role (IfATE, 2018). The context of the national curriculum for the education of the apprentice police constable has been developed within the overall professional context of the national apprenticeship standard.

Police constable apprenticeship curriculum: a professional overview

The national curriculum for the police constable apprentice has been developed so that the apprentice will receive a comprehensive professional education. It is based upon the professional responsibility of the police service and all who work within it to serve and protect the public in the most effective ways possible. This aligns the police with other professions that they deal with in the role of a police officer, such as social workers and solicitors, who require a degree for their role.

The prescribed three-year apprenticeship curriculum is professionally transformative, covering a breadth, depth and range of professional education for the police constable. This includes new curriculum content not present in previous national specifications of the training required to perform this policing role. It is an important development that police officers will receive dynamic information and training throughout their policing career.

The PEQF curriculum includes comprehensive, modern and up-to-date coverage of areas of knowledge, skills and behaviours that have been identified as critical to the twenty-first-century policing role of the constable. These include (but are not limited to):

- valuing diversity and inclusion;
- evidence-based policing;
- decision-making and discretion;
- crime prevention;
- proactive approaches to vulnerability;
- risk and public protection;
- supporting victims and witnesses of crime;
- well-being and resilience;
- digital policing.

Furthermore, the structure of the curriculum provides the apprentice with opportunities to engage in advanced learning and development and professional experience associated with key professional areas of policing (response policing; policing communities; policing the roads; information and intelligence; conducting investigations), in accordance with the operational requirements of the employing force.

In the widest educational context, the professional benefits of the apprenticeship education extend well beyond the confines of the curriculum itself, embracing the higher-level skills that a degree-based educational approach can import to the profession of policing. The PEQF programmes ensure that police constables will become more capable problem solvers, communicators, negotiators and leaders. Another benefit to the police constable will be an increasingly socially and emotionally intelligent individual in the performance of their professional role. The policing landscape is changing and so must the role of a police officer.

The content of the police constable apprenticeship curriculum can be stratified under three overarching headings of professional education and practice, as follows.

1. Learning and development applicable across a comprehensive range of policing professional situations and contexts

Learning and development enable the apprentice to do the following.

- Understand the legal and professional responsibilities of policing as a profession and modern policing strategies. Crime is changing, communities change and the police service and how it operates is under more forensic scrutiny than ever before. The main aim is to give new police officers the opportunity to be involved in developing new policing strategies in a contemporary policing landscape.

- Employ an ethical approach to policing, maintaining the highest professional standards when providing a service to the public. Social media has had a huge impact on how the police carry out their role as the public regularly film how police officers operate within their role. Conversely, the introduction of body-worn cameras being used by police officers on duty has been a welcome addition to police equipment in support of the police on duty. Body-worn cameras are regularly used in court and in investigations to support the actions and decisions made by police officers on duty.

- Proactively entrenching equality, diversity and human rights considerations as a core function of professional practice so that the police can appropriately serve our diverse communities.

- Acquire and apply appropriate research skills with the intention to put evidence-based policing initiatives into practice. Your research can have a huge impact on policing and communities; this could be an incredible opportunity to really make a difference to people's lives, communities and nationally.

- Understand, utilise and evaluate evidence-based initiatives in the context of preventative policing and problem-solving.

- Make decisions, founded upon critical thinking, in complex professional situations and contexts, demonstrating appropriate knowledge and application of powers, legislation and authorised professional practice (APP) (College of Policing, 2022c).
- Exercise autonomy and professional discretion, as appropriate to the role.
- Acquire, use and enhance professional communication and engagement skills, including effective use of digital-based communication.
- Apply conflict management skills, as appropriate and required.
- Acquire and demonstrate leadership, team working and partnership working skills in a policing context.
- Develop and maintain professional resilience in dealing with challenging situations.
- Apply techniques to manage their own well-being and that of other colleagues in the police service.
- Actively engage in continual self-reflection, evolving strategies to improve own professional practice.

Acquisition and confirmation of the above cross-cutting knowledge areas/skills sets are essential in ensuring that police constables can discharge their duties and responsibilities effectively. It is equally important in determining and underpinning the professional approach by which they can fulfil these duties and responsibilities.

2. Learning and development enabling the police constable to perform effectively in key specific areas of professional policing responsibility

Learning and development enable the apprentice to do the following.

- Apply knowledge of crime prevention techniques and initiatives when dealing with communities. It is imperative that the police work with the community to cut crime and offer crime prevention advice by being visible in the community. This builds confidence in the police; one major complaint from communities is the lack of visible presence on the streets by police officers.
- Understand and act upon the fundamental responsibility of the police service to identify and provide professional support to those who are vulnerable and at risk, whatever the context.
- Proactively identify, protect and support individuals in need of public protection, and deal professionally with those who perpetrate offences against them.
- Understand and engage in effective digital policing, with specific reference to digital-related crime.
- Understand national strategies in relation to counteracting terrorism and perform the front-line role of the police constable in this specific context.

Understand the criminal justice system as relevant to the role of the police constable, ensuring effective performance in relation to key criminal justice procedures and processes and providing appropriate support to victims and witnesses. An important aspect in effective policing is how you deal and support victims of crime. You will undergo intensive and detailed training in this area, which will be present in many of your modules that you will study at university as part of your apprenticeship programme.

3. Learning and development specifically and directly relevant to professional performance in core areas of policing

The educational spine of the curriculum is provided by progressive learning, development and professional practice in five core areas of policing practice integral to the performance of the police constable role, as follows:

- response policing;
- communities policing;
- policing the roads;
- information and intelligence;
- conducting investigations.

Although organisational structures and operational deployments will vary between forces, the above have been identified as resource-intensive areas of policing, viewed from the operational perspective and involvement of the police constable. You will study and learn in detail the above areas of core policing.

Learning and development enables the apprentice to:

- engage in lawful, safe and effective front-line policing in the specific professional areas of response policing, policing communities, policing the roads, information and intelligence and conducting investigations;
- research, develop, implement and review practical, evidence-based initiatives to improve policing performance in these areas and in doing so contribute themselves to the evolving evidence base for effective policing.

Starting the apprenticeship

After successfully completing all the recruitment stages to the police, you will be vetted in areas of work history, whether you have a criminal record and your financial security. You will also undergo a fitness test to ensure that you are fit enough to carry out the role of a police officer. You will be notified when all checks are complete and if successful you will then be offered a place on a PEQF study pathway after a check of your qualifications held. After accepting the job offer, you will be invited to a welcome/induction day where you will be asked to provide evidence of your qualifications and an ID check will be carried out. You will be asked to read and sign an apprenticeship learning agreement that outlines the employment arrangements between you and the police at the start of your apprenticeship. This also triggers the funding for your apprenticeship to pay for your programme of study. You will be notified by your university to enrol on your programme of study. It is extremely important that when enrolling at university that you pay particular attention when completing the online enrolment when they ask you to disclose if you have any learning requirements or disabilities. If you require extra support, you must inform the university so that arrangements can be put in place for you when your academic programme starts. You must also inform the police as well, so that support and any adjustments can be put in place to help you when on duty.

Day one of your apprenticeship

A typical day one (which varies with each employing force) will involve a welcome induction to the police force at training school or at your university. You will be welcomed to the force and given important information regarding your new role and given your new police uniform. You will also receive an input from the university that will be collaborating with your police force, giving you an overview of your programme of study. You may spend the first couple of weeks with your force where you will undergo specific police training such as personal safety and first aid courses before starting at university. The PCDA programme of study will be delivered by both police training staff and academic staff at the university to ensure that you get expert knowledge in academic and operational areas.

TASK

- During your first-day induction with the police, make a note of key personnel that you may have to contact at both the police force and university.

The PCDA training programme focuses on practical learning and is specifically designed to prepare you for your new role as a police officer, including areas such as searching and arresting suspects. There will be also classroom-based learning, often called learning blocks, throughout your apprenticeship, which will teach you the skills and knowledge required to be a police officer. After completing a learning block, you will then go out on rotation (on duty with the police) to put your new knowledge into practice with the public. From day one of your apprenticeship, you are employed as a police officer and will spend most of your time on the front-line with experienced officers. You will hear the term 'learning on the job' regularly during your time on the PCDA. The PCDA is an excellent structured programme where you will learn new skills in small learning blocks and then spend time on rotation perfecting these new skills and achieving operational competencies. When successfully complete in these areas, you will move on to the new learning block and operational rotation.

University programme

Your programme will consist of university learning blocks or modules, which will vary in length depending on the subject matter. You will receive the required information and knowledge for your role as a police officer. In addition, you will learn about the role, law and specific areas of policing that you will be dealing with on your next operational work placement rotation.

Your inputs will be delivered both by the police and university academic staff in a blended style of delivery. You will have teaching sessions in a classroom, which is called 'face-to-face delivery'; during the Covid-19 pandemic the majority of learning was online and some will remain online. You will also be expected to carry out self-directed distance learning. As with all university programmes, you are expected to carry out independent study and research away from designated timetabled sessions. In the next chapter, we will discuss the importance of time management and planning for study time and assessments. Your initial period of learning will be longer in length than other learning blocks as you will be taught the necessary knowledge required before you go on active duty. After your initial learning block, the learning blocks will be more subject specific, such as on investigation or response. You will move round to different areas of policing and be tutored by police experts in that area and put the theory that you have learnt into practice.

Assessments

Each module that you study at university will have specific learning outcomes that you must achieve to complete and successfully pass that module. The minimum pass mark for modules is 40 per cent; any grade lower than this is deemed to be a fail and the module will have be retaken. The final assessment, the EPA, has a higher pass mark of 50 per cent (the research project is included in this at 50 per cent).

How will I be assessed?

Assessment methods will assess your knowledge, understanding, skills, attitude and behaviour and will include:

- written assignments/reports/essays;
- presentations;
- self-reflection accounts;
- work-based portfolio of work activity;
- exams (online and written);
- role plays and scenarios;
- tabletop exercises;
- academic posters;

- case study exercises;
- professional discussions;
- evidence-based research project (EBRP).

Your apprenticeship is linked to a professional standard expected of a police officer and a Professional Policing degree, so all modules must be passed to complete the programme. You cannot progress to the next stage until all have been successfully passed and completed. You will need to complete both operational and university modules to progress to the next level and year of your programme. You are also required to obtain Independent Patrol Status (IPS) and complete an Operational Competence Portfolio (OCP); you will then achieve Full Operational Competence (FOC). This will be discussed in more detail later in this chapter.

TASK

Every police officer is required on appointment to be attested by making a declaration in a prescribed form before a Justice of the Peace in the force area they will police.

- What is the police constable oath?
- Why is it important that you understand the oath before committing to it?
- Research the Police (Conduct) Regulations 2008 and read the schedule of behaviours you must adhere to after stating the oath.

TASK

Degree classifications

- Research the following degree classification boundaries in your course handbook. This information will be available online contained in your module information on the virtual online environment (VLE).

Grade	Classification?
70+	
60–69	
50–59	
40–49	
0–39	

It is important that you strive to achieve the highest classification for your degree; aim high. With dedicated study and application, you can achieve high grades and a real sense of achievement. You have passed the entry criteria for the programme so you can achieve the grade you aspire to. I say to all my students: what work you put in often reflects your final grade.

Support at university

You will be assigned a personal tutor who will be your dedicated tutor for the duration of your course. They will support and guide you through your programme and you can contact them if you require advice and guidance. You will have regular meetings with your personal tutor and can arrange meetings with them as required. There is also lots of support available from other academic staff who can assist you with any programme queries and support if required. Module leaders will manage each module that you study and will be your first contact point for any questions you may have regarding the module and assessment queries. Your PCDA programme will have a course leader who you can contact for overall programme questions. An invaluable resource that is often overlooked is the university library and staff. Your faculty librarian can help you source required information and books for your programme.

Support from the police

There are dedicated staff who can help and assist you on your apprenticeship journey when you are on your work-based placements with the police. When you first start with the police, you will be allocated a named staff member for your cohort who will deliver police training. They will be your first point of contact for any questions you may have regarding your new role. There will be various members of staff that you will have regular contact with, such as training sergeants and inspectors who will manage the training department for your force. When you undergo your initial induction and training with your police force, you will be informed of the many support networks available to you. When on your operational rotations, you will be assigned a tutor who will support you when on duty when you put your new knowledge into practice.

Professional development of the police constable apprentice

An essential element of the degree-based education for the police constable role is the professional practice progression achieved during the various stages of your apprenticeship. This is a professional degree very much founded upon effective professional performance as an integral part of the academic achievement of the degree itself. The benefits of the PCDA are that the programme builds from very basic, introductory knowledge to more complex information and theory. It is important from the onset that you seek support and guidance if there are any issues or if you do not understand topic areas or information that you are taught. Some students do not ask for help and this can cause them to fall behind with their studies; we will cover strategies for effective studying on the programme in the next chapter. You must remember throughout your apprenticeship that all staff involved are invested in you successfully completing your programme. There is a wealth of support available to you; you just need to ask.

The apprenticeship curriculum has been carefully structured so that professional development proceeds at an appropriate pace alongside the educational achievement of the apprentice. The acquisition of operational experience on an ongoing basis also enables you to work independently to begin gathering evidence from your operational work. This is important, especially at the end of your apprenticeship, as it is evidence that will underpin confirmation of your competence in your role. It is very important that you are organised and plan your study blocks, identifying any areas for improvement during self-reflection.

The following summarises the various stages of professional development to be achieved by you during your three years of education and professional practice during your apprenticeship.

Apprenticeship Year 1: initial professional development

Education of the apprentice during the first year of the apprenticeship is set at academic level 4 and is founded upon the areas of education and professional practice specified previously. During your first year of academic study, you will be taught a range of academic and study skills to successfully achieve your academic programme.

A key stage in your professional development during your apprenticeship will therefore be the achievement of IPS. This is when you can demonstrate sufficient competence in your role to function independently, safely and lawfully in the workplace, alongside other policing colleagues in the operational arena.

The College of Policing recognises that there needs to be a degree of flexibility in the designation of the IPS threshold, in acknowledgement of the differing operational capabilities of local forces. Forces must provide practical opportunities for you to acquire the relevant skills. This will also consider the flexible educational partnership arrangements that have been entered into between apprenticeship forces and educational providers from the higher education sector.

The College of Policing has set a benchmark of professional development to the effect that the police constable apprentice must have achieved IPS no later than the end of the first year of their apprenticeship. In other words, IPS is being identified as a 'progression gateway' into Year 2 of the apprenticeship, alongside successful completion of the first year of degree study. Completing IPS successfully is a significant first milestone for you as you are now deemed to have sufficient experience and knowledge to attend jobs without a tutor supporting you.

Upon your achievement of IPS you will be eligible to acquire more specific practical experience in the workplace via professional deployments. Such professional deployments (which will continue right through to the end of your second apprentice year) should be related to the five areas of professional functionality that have been specified as core to the performance of the police constable role, namely response policing, community policing, policing the roads, information and intelligence, and conducting investigations.

Academic progression in Year 1 will be assessed through successful completion of all first-year degree modules, including elements of practical professional performance as part of the process. Due to the progression requirements, it is very important to seek support early if you are struggling in any modules and learning at university. Your module leader can support you and signpost you to specific support staff if required.

Apprenticeship Year 2: continuing professional development

The second year of your apprenticeship represents a major step forward in the development of a highly skilled, multi-competent police constable. Many of the key educational areas of the curriculum (both those of more generic policing relevance and also those more directly linked to specific policing functions and responsibilities) are covered in full by the end of Year 2. The learning and development covered by the second year of the apprenticeship curriculum is set at academic level 5.

Throughout Year 2, you will undertake more advanced learning across the five principal areas of professional practice, making use of the opportunities afforded by the framework and timeframe of the apprenticeship system to acquire higher-level operational knowledge and skills in these areas:

- response policing;
- policing communities;
- policing the roads;
- information and intelligence;
- conducting investigations.

This new deeper knowledge will be reinforced by practical experience achieved through operational deployment in your operational rotations with the police. It is vitally important that your academic learning is practice based, contextualised and further developed through operational rotations.

The preferred professional approach is that you will have achieved significant, identifiable deployment rotations across all five of the identified areas of professional practice by the end of the second year. This will provide maximum opportunity for identifying and developing knowledge and skills you may possess in relation to the abilities required for these operational roles. It is also an excellent time to reflect on whether you have any areas of police operations that you would like to specialise in when you have completed your probation.

The College of Policing have recognised that some forces will not have the organisational structures or operational capacity to offer significant deployment rotations across all five core areas. The curriculum has been designed in such a way to recognise the frequent overlapping nature of these professional functions and the fact that practical professional development can be achieved in a multiplicity of professional contexts. For example, the practical requirements for response policing may be achieved in a community policing context.

The professional requirement for your police force employer is that they must ensure that you are offered practical opportunities afforded by professional deployments to complete your required operational competencies. You will be provided with sufficient opportunities during Year 2 to achieve the more practice-based elements of the national curriculum. It is important that if you identify any gaps in your required knowledge that you speak to your supervisor and a bespoke plan can be put into place for you.

To progress into your final year, you will need to have demonstrated adequate knowledge, understanding and professional application in all level 5 learning undertaken during your second year. This will be measured through successful completion of all second-year degree modules, incorporating elements of practical professional performance. You must have achieved Full Operational Competence (FOC) by the end of Year 2.

Apprenticeship Year 3: advanced professional development

By the end of Year 2, you will have a meeting with the police to discuss what area of policing you will be assigned to in Year 3. You may be offered the opportunity to state your preference, but it may be decided by the operational need of your police force. It will be a placement of advanced learning and development and professional practice in one of the five core areas as listed in the bulleted list above for Year 2.

This provides an opportunity for the police to review your professional performance to date, the knowledge and skills acquired, and the professional behaviours demonstrated throughout your apprenticeship. What should also be discussed at this time is your professional career aspirations after you have successfully completed your apprenticeship. This professional discussion will also enable the employing force to make appropriate deployment decisions in accordance with their resourcing and staffing needs.

During Year 3, you will undertake advanced (at academic level 6) learning, development and professional practice associated with your chosen specialism, which will necessitate a significant deployment in that particular policing context.

In Year 3 you will also undertake learning and development at level 6, with reference to the following:

- evidence-based policing/problem-solving/research skills;
- leadership and teamworking;
- understanding the police constable role;
- communication skills;
- coaching, mentoring and assessment. The aim of this area of the curriculum is to equip you with the required skills and knowledge to coach and mentor new recruits to the police service. This will likely happen after you have successfully completed your probation and have gained substantial policing experience.

Your final assessment in Year 3 is the formal EPA, which consists of a professional discussion, based upon an Operational Competence Portfolio (OCP), together with completion of a work-related evidence-based research project. This research project has a written report element and a reflective component in the form of a presentation. You will undergo a panel discussion, which will be attended by the Independent Assessor, a police representative from your force and a university representative who is likely to be your research project supervisor.

Successful completion of the degree in Professional Policing Practice is integrated into the EPA. Completion of the EPA will enable the employer force to confirm the apprentice in post, as having successfully completed probation.

An apprentice who successfully undertakes advanced learning and development in the field of conducting investigations will complete all the necessary learning and development relating to achievement of Professionalising Investigation Programme (PIP) 2, which can be evidenced in their OCP. Completion of the PCDA (investigative pathway) enables the apprentice to receive PIP 1 and 2 accreditation, subject to successful completion of the appropriate assessment and portfolio.

An apprentice who wishes to be accredited as a PIP 2 investigator must have passed the national investigators' exam. It can be completed during the PCDA, but should not detract from the apprentice's primary goal to successfully achieve the apprenticeship.

An apprentice who successfully completes Year 1 and 2 (level 4 and 5) of the PCDA will have achieved the requisite learning for the role of intelligence support officer (ISO). Accreditation in this role is based on successful completion of the assessment criteria relating to the ISO role in the OCP. Successful completion of the intelligence specialism in Year 3 provides the learner with the pre-requisite learning to progress towards the roles of intelligence officer, researcher or analyst.

Graduation

After completion of your programme and final sign-off from the police you will have a graduation ceremony to celebrate your achievement. This may be held at police premises or at the university and is a special event. You will be able to invite your family and friends to share your special day of achievement. You will wear a cap and gown that is specific to each university and enjoy a day that you will always remember.

> ### CASE STUDY
>
> The chapters of this book follow the learner journey of student officer Peter Morris from day 1 when he started the PCDA through to his EPA at the end of Year 3. This case study will give you an overview of a typical learner journey of a police officer apprentice.

PC 3001 Peter Morris started his PCDA journey three years ago following a change of career after working in the pub industry for ten years. Since leaving school, he had always aspired to join the police but his local police force was not recruiting at that time and he was offered a job in business development for a large pub chain. When the 'Boris uplift' was announced in 2019, at the age of 30, he decided to apply to a large Midlands police force and was offered a place on the PCDA programme. After successfully completing the recruitment process, he attended the induction evening with the police two weeks before his start date with the police.

He was anxious before the induction evening because he thought he would be the oldest member of the group and was very apprehensive about starting a degree course at 30. He had not been in education for many years and was worried about returning to study after such a significant period of time. Peter was also concerned that apprenticeships were only for school leavers and that he would struggle with the age gap with other student officers in the group. When he arrived at the police headquarters for the induction evening, he was relieved that there was a wide range of age groups in his cohort. There was a diverse range of people from all walks of life who would bring an array of skills and experience to the police. During the evening there were presentations from the police, detailing their new role and expectations of joining the police. There was also a presentation from the course leader from the university at which he would be studying for his degree programme. Peter felt at ease when the university programme was discussed and what support was available to all students to successfully complete the programme. He was also very happy when it was discussed with the group why police education and training had changed and the reasons why change was needed. He was also reassured to learn that all the training that he would undertake during the three years of his probation would be recognised and if successful he would be awarded a degree in Professional Policing Practice at the end of his programme. The police would fully fund the degree and he would be paid a monthly salary throughout the whole PCDA programme.

The format of the PCDA was discussed in detail and a timetable was given to all attendees for Year 1 of the programme. He was very relieved that the programme included time at university where he would learn the essential knowledge he required to be a police officer, such as law and procedure. When he was not at university, he would be on an operational work placement putting all his new skills and knowledge to the test when he was on police duty with his tutor. When Peter left the induction evening at the police headquarters, he felt very reassured and excited at the prospect of starting his new career as a student officer with the police.

To be continued in Chapter 3...

Conclusion

There has been a significant change in how police education is delivered to new-recruit police officers due to the new challenges and complexities demanded of the role. The new PEQF entry routes offer new opportunities for applicants who may not have considered a career within the police and attending university. Planning and preparing before and during your PCDA programme will ensure that you have the required information and insight to complete your degree apprenticeship successfully. This important planning for your apprenticeship programme will ensure that you successfully complete your degree in Professional Policing Practice, achieve your operational competencies and pass your probation. You will then be confirmed as a substantive police officer and attend a graduation to celebrate your achievements.

Further reading

College of Policing (2020) *Policing in England and Wales Future Operating Environment 2040*. [online] Available at: https://assets.college.police.uk/s3fs-public/2020-08/Future-Operating-Environment-2040-Part1-Trends.pdf (accessed 15 November 2022).

Pepper, I, Brown, I and Stubbs, P (2021) A Degree of Recognition Across Policing: Embedding a Degree Apprenticeship Encompassing Work-based Research. *Journal of Work-Applied Management*, 14(1). [online] Available at: www.emerald.com/insight/content/doi/10.1108/JWAM-12-2020-0056/full/html (accessed 10 November 2022).

Quality Assurance Agency for Higher Education (QAA) (2018) *UK Quality Code, Advice and Guidance: Work-based Learning*. [online] Available at: www.qaa.ac.uk/quality-code/advice-and-guidance/work-based-learning (accessed 16 November 2022).

3 The PCDA support triangle

> **LEARNING OBJECTIVES**
>
> After reading this chapter you will be able to:
>
> - understand the importance of working collaboratively with your employer and training provider to successfully complete your apprenticeship;
> - discuss the positive aspects of tripartite review meetings and how the police and university can support you in the workplace and at university;
> - explain the importance of implementing effective study and academic skills when producing academic work for submission at university.

Introduction

Working together as a team is fundamental to successfully completing your apprenticeship. This chapter covers the importance of good relationships with both the police as your employer and with your training provider, the university. There is a wealth of support and expertise available to you to support and guide you through your apprenticeship, whether it is when you are on duty or when you are writing an assignment.

The triangle in Figure 3.1 demonstrates that your PCDA comprises three elements – you as a student officer, your university and the police. To successfully complete your apprenticeship, all parties in the PCDA triangle must work together to ensure that you have the opportunities and support to guide you through the process. You have a part to play as well by ensuring that you complete your force operational competencies and successfully complete your academic programme to the best of your ability. When all is successfully complete and achieved, you can then undertake your final assessment – the end-point assessment (EPA).

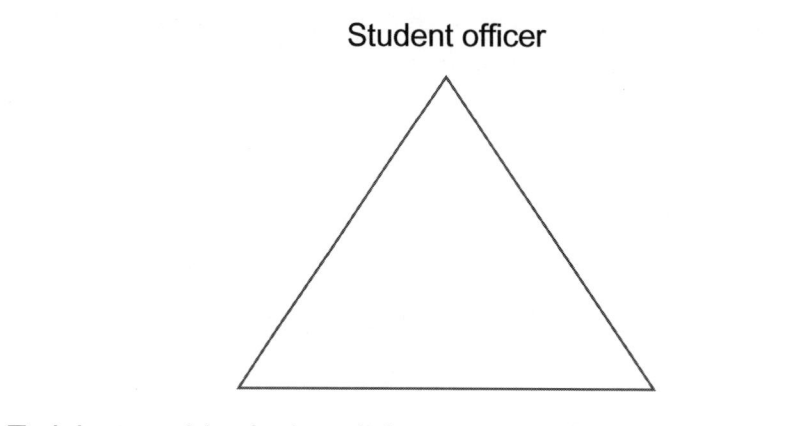

Figure 3.1 *The PCDA support and learning triangle*

The benefits of your apprenticeship

Learning through an apprenticeship is a new concept in policing and will open up a wealth of new opportunities to develop skills and knowledge not available previously in the old regime of police training. As a policing apprentice, you will:

- learn practical skills on the job such as arresting offenders and searching them;
- gain crucial and specific experience on a rotational basis in different areas of operational policing;
- develop essential learning tools such as communication and personal safety techniques;
- learn and develop study and academic skills at level 6;
- earn crucial qualifications that will be recognised after you leave the police.

The PCDA will open up many opportunities to you as a learner as you will gain a qualification in policing, which will lead to further opportunities for the future. It is important to note that when you have completed your apprenticeship, employers will be confident that you have the skills and training needed to be able to do the job. Your training will allow you to demonstrate basic skills, including English and maths, teamwork and health and safety awareness, as well as more specialised capabilities such as investigation to help you progress your career in policing.

Expectations of your PCDA programme

Joining the police can be a difficult journey starting from your application to finally being offered a role as a student officer with your chosen police force. It is a difficult and challenging job and your programme of study and time on duty will often push you way out of your comfort zone. This will develop you as a person and often when you look back to the start of your programme you will see how you have developed personally and professionally. You must have the correct positive mindset when starting your apprenticeship and you must expect that you will encounter difficult times such as dealing with victims of crime and long shifts. You must also be prepared and ready for your academic studies, which will equip you with the required knowledge for your role. As with any job you must undergo training before you are expected to carry out the role, and this is no different. There is a lot of information to learn and assimilate before you go out on your first duty with your tutor. All the training and knowledge that you acquire during your apprenticeship is necessary for your role and must be completed. A real benefit of any apprenticeship programme is that the journey is tailored and bespoke to you. This chapter covers how each student officer is supported throughout the PCDA by the police and the university. If you require extra support, that will be implemented and an individual learning plan will be put in place to support and guide you through the PCDA.

Most apprenticeships as well as the PCDA include the following elements.

- **A competencies element** – this demonstrates that you are competent in performing the role of an operational PC and you will produce a portfolio of evidence to prove this.
- **A technical knowledge element** – this is your programme of study at university. It demonstrates that you have the necessary technical skills, knowledge and understanding of theoretical concepts as well as knowledge and understanding of law and the role of a police constable.
- **Key skills element** – this demonstrates that you are competent in areas such as teamwork, problem-solving and communication, which is essential in policing.

Equality of opportunity for all students and available support when on the PCDA

As an apprentice and an employee of the police service, you are protected by law in the workplace. The Equality Act 2010 protects people from discrimination, harassment and victimisation in and out of the workplace.

TASK

- What are the nine characteristics that are protected by the Equality Act 2010?
- Why is it important that employees have legal protection in the workplace?
- What can be the impact on the individual if they are discriminated against or bullied at work?
- What support is available to you at both the university and police if you feel that you are being discriminated against in the workplace?

Under the Equality Act 2010, if you have a disability or an additional need you are protected by this legislation provided you disclose this information at the time of your application. Sometimes you may not be aware and may encounter some issues when you start your degree – you can raise this and if deemed necessary you can undergo tests, such as a dyslexia test. If you undergo a screening or test and it is found that you require support, then this can be implemented in the workplace and at university.

The term 'additional learning needs' (ALNs) refers to people who, for a variety of reasons, may face barriers to education and learning, which can have an impact if they are not offered additional support. It is very important that you disclose this information to the police and the university if you have any additional learning requirements so that a bespoke support plan can be implemented for you. There is no need to be embarrassed about asking for help; many police officers have ALNs and have a very successful career in the police. Within your cohort, it will be very likely that there will be around five other student officers who require extra support with their studies. If unsure, you must tell your personal tutor who will start the process and get you booked in for the relevant screening.

Please see Table 3.1 for some information about ALNs that are very commonplace in the workplace and university.

Table 3.1 Some common examples of barriers to learning which may require support in the workplace

Dyslexia	It is estimated that one in ten of the population is dyslexic. Learners may demonstrate difficulties with reading and spelling, remembering and processing information.
Dyspraxia	Sometimes known as developmental co-ordination disorder (DCD), it is thought to affect around 5 per cent of the population. Learners may have some difficulties with physical co-ordination, special awareness, balance and completing some practical tasks.
Dyscalculia	It is estimated that up to 6 per cent of the population may be affected by dyscalculia. Learners will have difficulties with numbers, counting and calculation.
Dysgraphia	Learners have difficulty executing handwriting and writing legibly and fluently.
Autism spectrum condition (ASC)	A lifelong condition that affects how a person relates to and communicates with other people and makes sense of the world around them. ASC is an overarching term used to describe autism and Asperger's syndrome.
Attention deficit disorder (ADD)/attention deficit (hyperactivity) disorder (ADHD)	Estimates suggest that around 4 per cent of children may have ADHD. Learners may have difficulty with concentrating, organisation and focus. They may be easily distracted, restless and change activity or task regularly.

If it has been identified that you require additional learning support, it may be provided on a one-to-one basis by specialist tutors depending on the individual need and requirement. Alternatively, you may be offered the following forms of support.

- Extra guidance and support provided by a vocational tutor or skills coach.
- Extra time in written and online examinations.
- The police may offer specialist software for your computer at work and support in writing statements and completing paperwork.
- A learning contract that has been approved by the university that notifies markers to be mindful and consider that there may be minor errors in grammar and spelling in the submission.
- Additional time provided to complete assignment work or learning modules.
- More frequent, bespoke progress reviews to monitor progress.
- Allocation of a learning mentor to develop study skills or support social and emotional needs.
- Close monitoring by the shift sergeant or tutor constable.
- Specific information, advice and guidance provided by university student support colleagues.

You must inform both the police and university if you have any areas in which you need further support. Learning support funding is available to meet the costs of implementing reasonable adjustments for apprentices with a learning difficulty or disability where this affects their ability to continue and complete their apprenticeship.

Tripartite meetings

Your first tripartite meeting will take place shortly after you start your apprenticeship. They are regular meetings that will occur approximately every 12 weeks to check on your current progress on your apprenticeship programme. They are called tripartite meetings as there will be three people in the meeting – you, a member of university staff (usually your work-based coach) and a representative from the police (normally your tutor or supervisor). These are mandatory throughout your PCDA programme and are important as they check that you are on track with your progress and achieving your targets. They will identify areas of strength and any areas where you may need extra support. This is also an opportunity for you to discuss your progress with university and police staff and get feedback. During these meetings you will set targets for the next three months for both university and police work. You will also work through the mandatory knowledge, skills and behaviours (KSBs) which you need to complete successfully to finish your apprenticeship.

Your first tripartite meeting will involve an initial assessment discussion, which will cover information that you shared with the university when you enrolled or during your induction week. This will take the form of a professional discussion which will explore your current confidence and competency, your background and experience. You will also discuss any qualifications that you have already achieved to date. If you have not achieved level 2 in English and maths, a discussion will take place regarding how you will achieve these qualifications as they are a mandatory element to passing your apprenticeship. Together with your work-based coach and the police representative, a judgement will be made regarding your plan of learning. This plan of learning will be bespoke and personalised individually to you as this is your learning journey. Even though all PCDA students will undergo the same training, they will have different learning plans and targets.

The role of the police as your employer

The role of the police representative in tripartite reviews is essential. Your tutor or supervisor will be best placed to make judgements about your knowledge, skills and behaviours in the workplace and practical application when on duty with the public. They will observe first-hand the impact your training is having when you are on your rotation. Your tutor or supervisor will be able to identify any strong skill sets you are displaying and may give you additional responsibilities or opportunities to experience specialist operations or attachments. They will also identify any gaps in your knowledge and if required give extra support when you are on duty.

The role of the work-based coach

When you start your academic programme at university, you will be assigned a work-based coach who will support and guide you through your PCDA programme. They will be representing you on behalf of the university at your tripartite meeting. Your work-based coach will be your first point of call for any general apprenticeship programme queries and will keep a close eye on your progress on the PCDA. They will chair the tripartite meeting and will take notes and complete your tripartite review paperwork after the meeting has concluded. Your work-based coach will liaise with the police if there are any arising issues or if you fall behind with university work or require extra support.

Items that will be discussed in your tripartite meeting

Examples of topics discussed in your tripartite meeting are as follows:

- how you are and how you are progressing since your last meeting;
- upcoming assignments and tasks;
- grades obtained;
- KSBs signed off;
- percentage of your IPS/FOC completed;
- any resubmissions of work;
- any learning support or extra guidance required;
- feedback from university staff and the police;

- off-the-job tracker completion;
- anything that is occurring in your home/personal life that both parties need to be aware of to implement extra support if required;
- British values in the tripartite;
- set targets/plan of action for the next three months until your next review meeting.

Table 3.2 (see pages 36–7) is an example of some of the areas covered in a tripartite review.

What is off-the-job training?

As well as receiving training at work with the police where you will perform duties as a police officer, you will also complete regular off-the-job training (OTJT) included as part of your working hours. OTJT will help you develop the new KSBs which you are required complete for your apprenticeship to be signed off as complete. You may receive up to 20 per cent OTJT over the duration of your police apprenticeship (it is likely to be higher than this depending on your employer/higher education institution collaboration).

The Education and Skills Funding Agency (ESFA) (2022a) and the government (HM Government, 2022c) have produced clear guidelines on what can be counted towards apprentices' minimum entitlement to OTJT in normal working hours.

- The teaching of theory – in your university learning blocks you will attend lectures, role plays and complete online learning.
- Practical training – shadowing, mentoring and training in specialist areas of policing.
- Learning support and time spent writing assessments and assignments.

Your work-based coach will explain how to complete the OTJT tracker and give you a template to record all your OTJT hours at each tripartite meeting. These are then recorded and uploaded onto your apprenticeship record. You will have learning/training blocks of varying length with the police/university depending on where you are in your initial training. At the start of your programme, you could be at university/police training school for up to 15 weeks. There will be a wide range of delivery and attendance models, including face to face, online delivery or a blended learning approach. This will be recorded as OTJT and will need to be recorded on your OTJT tracker.

An area that is often misunderstood by a small minority of students is that assignment writing time and preparation is included in your learning time at university. Time will be set aside for you specifically in your learning block to do this. If you do not use this time effectively, you will have to do this work in your own time. When your programme was prepared, assignment preparation and time were carefully factored in due to the size of the task. Even though you are at university for the day or in a learning block, you are still getting paid for a working day with the police so you are expected to work the same hours as you would on shift with the police.

Table 3.2 An example of a typical review

REVIEW OF PROGRESS OF ELEMENTS OF APPRENTICESHIP STANDARD		Planned End Date	25.9.25
Area for review	**Comments and actions**		
English functional skills progress	100%	Exempt	
Maths functional skills progress	100%	Exempt	
Digital skills progress	Not part of standard	Exempt	
		Josh and I discussed access and usage of platforms required for the programme such as Blackboard, Teams, the Office suite and OneFile and he feels confident using these programs.	
Attendance and timekeeping	In work	Good	Satisfactory	Poor
	In university	Good	Satisfactory	Poor
Progress with qualification BSc (Hons) Professional Policing Practice	Aspirational grade: 1st	**Rotation 1 modules: Introduction to Communities** *Individual presentation (10 mins): 21.02.2023* *Reflective writing piece (1000 words): 21.02.2023* Josh has completed the essay for this rotation and is working on the PowerPoint presentation. He knows what is required for each submission and he has the assessment brief. Josh has done voice-overs before and while he has not enjoyed the process, he knows how to do this. Josh has raised concerns about the functionality of his microphone and while he may be able to find an alternative microphone, Josh may be able to book a room within Castle Heath Lane Library and IT Centre where there is a PC with video conferencing facilities, and this could be used to record his presentation if he cannot locate a microphone. Josh has also been given the advice to reach out to Stuart if he requires any further help or clarification. **PDP Jay Shaw** *Literature review (500 words): 28.02.23* This is another submission that Josh is working on now and he is thinking of conducting a literature review around the culture of drug use in universities as this is of interest to him and he has noticed a gap in the current literature. Josh has also been given the advice to reach out to Jay if he requires any further help or clarification.		

	Introduction to Policing Practice (Steve Jones) Summative test 1: 56% Summative test 2: 84% Summative test 3: 76% **What do you feel has gone well with your academic studies so far?** • Practical application – scenarios have been successful, especially in relation to legislation. • Group discussions – getting opinions from peers has really helped his understanding. • Volume of new learning has been enjoyable; however, the time frame made this challenging at times. **What needs to be developed by the university?** • More practical application once the foundation of knowledge has been taught will help to embed new learning. • The first distance learning week could have been done in the first topic; some elements were not appropriate for distance learning.	
Progress with any required additional qualification *Independent Patrol Status (IPS)*	Josh had not commenced his rotation at the time of the review and as such progression could not be discussed. We did, however, discuss the expectations and requirements of the IPS while he is in the community rotation. Josh is aiming for 35 per cent on the rotation, which is achievable as he is probably going to have a lot of response jobs during the Christmas period. If Josh hits the percentage target, this puts him in a good position to achieve IPS at the 40 weeks and one-day threshold. Josh's tutor is relatively new, and he is going to take Josh through the process of IPS/portfolio. Paul reinforced the need for protected learning but advised that for the first few weeks, Josh needs to focus on the job/competencies as this will help to build up evidence. Josh understands that he needs to use the IPS as a working document to clarify what evidence has been achieved. This needs to be done regularly and Josh needs to ensure he is taking ownership of his IPS progression and is using the IPS as a working document and the verification of evidence is being done regularly and not end loaded.	N/A *Rotation has not commenced*
Record any off-the-job learning undertaken in the workplace since the last review	Josh understands the need to engage with APTEM once he has access as the system logs his 'planned' off-the-job learning linked to his university session. Josh has been advised to wait for the user guides to be issued to the cohort to clarify the expectations of logging sessions in the system. Josh had a good understanding of the concept of off-the-job learning and the types of activities which could be classed as OTJL in his rotation. This 'unplanned' learning needs to be recorded on OneFile and evidence of this needs to be brought to the next scheduled tripartite meeting.	Planned: 11h 0m Unplanned: 0h **Total:** **11h**

TASK

- Check the following HM Government website for current OTJT information and make any notes that will help you: www.gov.uk/government/publications/apprenticeships-off-the-job-training.

Your tripartite meeting may take place at work or at university, and it could be face-to-face or online. You will be given adequate notice of the appointment and your work or university timetable will be checked to ensure that you are in work. The meeting will take around one hour. It is important that you are prepared to discuss your progress since your last review meeting and that you have completed your OTJT tracker. You will also be asked to discuss your progress towards any targets that you were set at your last review meeting.

SMART coaching and mentoring

When you meet with your work-based learning coach and police mentor you will discuss a variety of areas during the review. It will normally focus on some specific themes that you have had the opportunity to develop. This meeting can also be used to discuss areas where you agree a plan of action and training plan for the next review. This records your learning journey on your apprenticeship.

Table 3.3 An example of target setting at a tripartite review

Review of previous actions		
Targets	**Progress**	**Met/not met**
To maximise the use of protected learning time	Josh has finished assignments as he has completed a previous degree and understands the need to utilise time.	**Yes**/no
To make time for reading and to read around the core topics	As above. Josh is now using a flip book to refresh and recap PACE as he begins his rotation.	**Yes**/no
To link theory to practice	Josh has not begun rotation yet; some theory linked to role-play scenarios. Will complete on rotation starting in two weeks and feed back progress at next review.	**Yes**/no

More specific targets will be made using the SMART mnemonic.

- **S**pecific.
- **M**easurable.
- **A**chievable.
- **R**elevant (and realistic).
- **T**ime-bound.

Table 3.4 An example of a detailed action plan at a tripartite review

Action plan		
SMART milestone targets and actions	**How will target be achieved?**	**By when?**
To achieve a 1st in the PowerPoint, Reflective Writing and Literature Review submissions.	– Plan each submission and obtain support from module leads if required. – Clarify the criteria to achieve a 1st class grade. – Access VLE to access learning material appropriate to each submission.	28.02.2023
To document planned (APTEM) and unplanned (OneFile) off-the-job hours, linking to the knowledge, skills and behaviours of the apprenticeship standard.	– Access APTEM and update sessions which have been attended retrospectively. – Keep a log of new learning obtained through shadowing, observing etc and write as a journal in OneFile, documenting the new learning and how this relates to the apprenticeship standard. – Familiarise yourself with the apprenticeship standard. Available at: www.instituteforapprenticeships.org/apprenticeship-standards/police-constable-degree	17.02.2023
To conduct a safe and lawful arrest while on duty.	– Revise definitions in law to increase confidence while out on duty. – Utilise off-the-job learning to observe best practice of lawful arrests in a variety of situations. – Engage with tutor for the necessity of arrests on spontaneous arrests and use appropriate feedback as required.	31.01.2023
To evidence at least 35% of criteria in the Independent Patrol Status Portfolio.	– Familiarise yourself with the required criteria, focusing on the evidence which must be covered in this rotation. – Use IPS as a working document and update regularly. – Liaise with tutors to establish gaps and the most stable jobs to address these gaps in evidence.	17.02.2023
To gain an understanding of British Values within your role as a police officer.	– Research what British Values are and how this links in with the Prevent duty. You may find this link a useful starting point: www.youtube.com/watch?v=U9cqHsiE0vM – Reflect on how these strands relate to you as a police officer.	20.12.2022

TASK

British Values are embedded throughout your apprenticeship. During your review, you will be asked to discuss how you have incorporated these values into your apprenticeship. Research British Values and answer the following questions.

- What are British Values?
- Why are they important in your role as a police officer?
- Self-reflection – are there any gaps in your knowledge and how can you improve any areas of weakness?

Essential study skills to obtain top grades

Embarking on a new programme of study such as a degree at university can sometimes feel overwhelming and challenging. There are many new skills to develop such as academic writing and critical thinking skills. Many lines of support are available to help you develop the essential skills to navigate your degree programme and obtain the classification grade that you aspire to achieve. It is very important that you attend all timetabled lessons and any support sessions that you have been instructed to attend. If you are unsure of any areas, you should seek advice and guidance from your personal tutor or work-based coach.

Finding advice and support

All universities provide a range of academic writing support, and you are encouraged to access these invaluable sessions to perfect and get to grips with the art of academic writing. The sessions are usually offered through the library and offer support with other skills such as critical thinking skills and referencing. If you visit your library service online, you will find lots of information and guidance for study and academic skills. There will be regular workshops and online learning available to book on to that will run throughout the academic year. If you would rather arrange a face-to-face meeting and library tour, you can make an appointment to do this online or in person.

Study and academic skills

Writing essentials

There are three key components to successful academic writing.

1. **Relevance** – it is imperative that you understand the question or task that you have been asked to complete. If you are unsure of any aspect of your assessment, contact your module leader as soon as you can for guidance. A key

tip is to ensure that everything you write is relevant to the task posed. Many students make the mistake of writing an answer to a question that they would have liked instead. If you do not include the expected content of your question, you will be graded lower. Due to a strict word-count requirement, it is vital not to waste words on irrelevant material or unnecessary 'waffle'.

2. **Coherence** – it is very important that your piece of writing makes sense to the reader. Your submissions should have a clear purpose and direction and be written with a target reader in mind. If your work was picked up by a member of the public with no knowledge of the topic in policing, would they understand the message and be able to tell someone else about the key points of your work? Do not assume that it will be your lecturer marking your work and think, '*oh, they will know what I'm writing about so I will not have to explain or define that term*'; this is not good practice. You are showing to the marker that you do indeed understand the topic, and this is your opportunity to do so.

3. **Criticality** – most academic writing is 'critical writing', that is, it is analytical and evaluative rather than just descriptive. Many students try and 'tell a story' in their submissions, but the marker will not be able to award higher grades as the piece does not weigh up both sides of the story.

A basic requirement in writing assignments is to make it clear to the reader that you have understood the important concepts, theories and arguments in your topic area. In Year 1 of university, a basic level of intellectual engagement and understanding is sufficient to pass an assignment. Your first year at level 4 is the time to perfect your academic writing skills. However, as you progress through your policing degree, you will be increasingly assessed on your ability to demonstrate that you have approached concepts, theories and arguments with a critical view.

Preparing your work for submission

Is your work ready for final submission?

When university staff mark and grade your submitted work, they will refer closely to the assessment guidelines and marking descriptors. This information will be found in your assignment brief and in your module handbook for each module. You should read this information as this is what is required to pass the learning outcomes of the module. It is very important that you understand what is required for your assignment before starting your submission.

Top tips

- Have you followed the assignment brief guidelines on the required content, referencing, formatting and presentation?
- Have you answered the question posed in a concise, direct and appropriate way?
- Is the content relevant?

- Have you supported your content and ideas with credible sources and evidence?
- Is your referencing complete, accurate and consistent throughout your work?
- How/where do you need to submit your work? Online on the VLE or in person?
- Does your work need to be submitted anonymously, with no identifying names or student number included in your work?
- What is the submission date and time?

The importance of adhering to word-count requirements

If there is a stated word-count guide, it is very important that you follow the guidelines as you will be penalised if you fail to meet or exceed the specified word count. During assignment planning, a word count is allocated to ensure that all students have the same limit and that the assignment is equitable for all. Often written assignments need to be a certain length to ensure that you have adequate space to include a substantial amount of detail and argument. As you progress through your degree programme, you will find the word count increases as you move up to levels 5 and 6. They also require you to be selective in your judgement regarding the key aspects of the topic being covered. Word-count requirements will vary depending on the university you are studying at; some may give you a maximum word count that you must adhere to. Most universities will allow you a 10 per cent leeway, which means you can submit 10 per cent below or above the word count without being penalised. If your assessment states 2000 words (10 per cent = 200), you could submit 1800 or 2200 words without it affecting your overall grade.

The importance of checking and proofreading your final submission

Many students do not proofread or edit their work before submitting and this can cause a significant reduction in the grade for their work. It is very important that you read your draft a few times before submitting and remove/edit any anomalies present in your work. Spelling mistakes and sentences which make no sense will also be frowned on by your marker, often making it appear that the work has been rushed and is sloppy. All marking criteria will include guidance regarding spelling and grammar and there can be a significant drop in grade if you do not remove errors from your work before submission. It is often easier to print out your work and mark with a highlighter any errors that require amending. You need to check that your content flows and is in order. I would recommend that you ask a friend or family member to check your work too as sometimes it is hard to spot mistakes when you have been working on a piece for a considerable amount of time. If you have a learning contract in place, you could ask the module leader or a member of teaching/library staff to check your work. Also remember to add the details of your learning contact on the top sheet of your submission so that the marker is aware. Sometimes at level 4 you may be offered the opportunity to submit a draft to your module leader to check that you are on the correct lines before submitting. Use this invaluable service if available and incorporate the feedback given by the member of academic staff.

Formatting

You will be graded on the breath of your knowledge, critical analysis and clarity and coherence of your writing. You could submit a piece of work where the content is very good, but your marker will not be impressed if the presentation and format is poor. Submissions that have poor formatting can be difficult to navigate and read, which will have a negative effect on your overall grade. Be proud of the work that you submit and ensure it is clear, easy to read and professionally presented.

Guidance for assessment submissions

First impressions are very important when a marker begins to grade your work. The way your assignment looks demonstrates your approach to your studies. A well-presented submission shows that you are professional, pay attention to detail and are conscientious about your work. See below for some top tips to impress your marker.

Essays/written reports

Written assignments should have a title page on page one with clear information about the submission. This should include:

- your name/student ID number (or just student ID number if the assignment is to be submitted anonymously);
- the university you are studying at and your programme of study;
- the full title of your assignment;
- the module for which it is being written;
- date;
- module leader's name.

In your submission, the submission should include the following:

- word count;
- numbered pages;
- appropriate font and font size – academic work should be written in a font that is easy to read; this information should be in your assignment guidance or use standard fonts such as Times New Roman or Arial in size 11 or 12;
- a document that looks professional throughout;
- reference list/bibliography on last page(s).

Examination and assessment planning

Preparation is key and a positive mindset is important for achieving high grades in written exams and assignments. Exams test your ability to recall information and write under pressure. Written assignments test your knowledge in the topic area and having a clear strategy before you sit your exam will reap rewards in obtaining the grade that you have set a target for. At the start of each academic year, you will be given a designated exam and assessment week timetable so you can start to plan which of your modules are written assignments and examinations. At the start of each module, you will be given clear guidance on your questions or topics for assignments.

Exam preparation

Throughout your module, weekly sessions ensure that you complete all your pre-session tasks, including reading tasks, as you could be tested on anything contained in that module topic. If you have any specific questions or queries about the content, contact your lecturer by email or ask in class so that you have a clear understanding of all the content.

For each session, print out the slides and make notes as the lecture is delivered or make notes and type them up and place in a folder. If your notes are in bullet points, it really does help with revision. As your examination date gets nearer, start to make key bullet points on one A4 piece of paper for each topic area. Highlight key terms with a highlighter pen and read as often as you can. Give yourself at least four weeks (more if possible) to start to read through your module topics and revise for your forthcoming exam.

As with any written assignment, before you start writing, read the question posed carefully and highlight key terms. Write down any key points that you will need to include in your question at the side of your exam booklet, move on and have a look at the other questions. If you have a choice of questions, such as having to choose two out of five, decide which ones you definitely don't want to answer before deciding the two you will answer.

Top tips

- Give yourself five to ten minutes to read the exam guidance/instructions.
- Read the questions and read them again to ensure you fully understand the questions posed before attempting to answer them.
- Make it clear which question you are answering! You would be surprised how many students do not clearly label which question they are answering in the answer booklet.
- Work out the time you have for each question and stick to it. If you have not finished one question after your allocated time, move on to the next question but leave yourself space to come back to it if you finish the other questions in good time.
- Each answer should have a structure and be easy to read and understand for the marker. If your writing it very untidy and difficult to read, the marker will not be able to mark your work. This in turn will have a negative effect on your grade.

- The structure should be clear and written in paragraphs; one large chunk of written text can be difficult for a marker to read and grade.
- Anything that you do not want marked, any roughwork or points, should have a clear line drawn through it.
- In a long answer, stick to one point per paragraph and leave a line between paragraphs.
- Remember – make your marker's life easier with writing that flows and is easy to read with clear points. It might be one of 400 that they have to mark so be mindful that if it is difficult to read this will be reflected in your grade given.

Assessment preparation

Important: ensure you have made a note of the deadline of submission and time that your work must be submitted or uploaded. Many submissions now at university are through the VLE; ensure that you submit the correct work to the module and at the right submission point. You are responsible for submitting the correct work on the VLE; if a mistake is made, it cannot be rectified after the submission deadline and you could fail the module. You should receive a receipt for an online submission; always check that you have received this as it is evidence that you have submitted your work. If you do not receive one, you must contact IT or try to submit again – if your marker cannot access your work, it is an instant failure.

Key motivation tips for success

Sometimes your work–life balance can become challenging, but remember the following.

- You will succeed if you carefully plan and balance your work and apprenticeship programme.
- Prepare for your EPA early on in your programme so you are fully prepared and ready for your final assessment.
- You will gain a real sense of achievement and accomplishment when you successfully complete your apprenticeship and probation.
- You can start to consider/apply for areas of specialism within the police service.
- The police have made a huge investment in you to succeed and become a substantive police officer.
- You have learnt 'on the job' and gained invaluable experience in the four core areas of policing.
- Use the wealth of support available to you at university and in the workplace.
- Be honest if you require support and guidance; staff are specifically employed to support students.
- You will graduate with a degree in Professional Policing Practice.

> **CASE STUDY**
>
> Two weeks after PC Peter Morris attended his induction evening, he attended his first day at training school to embark on his new career as a police officer. He spent two days with the police where it was a whirlwind of new information regarding his new role, and he found it difficult to concentrate and take in all this new information and remember it. He then started at university for a 15-week period of classroom learning, which covered all the basics for his role as a police officer and the law to prepare him for his first operational placement on response.
>
> His programme of study comprised blended learning, consisting of three days at university and two days at home studying independently online. He found he was struggling to concentrate, especially when studying independently at home on his laptop all day. The words on the screen were difficult to read at times and he started to get frustrated as he was unable to retain the information he was reading. He was particularly worried as he had a knowledge check about legislation on the following Monday. Although he had left school 14 years ago, he remembered clearly that he had struggled to complete written work at school and had issues when sitting written examinations. Even though he had spoken to his teacher, his concerns were not taken seriously and he was offered no support in the classroom or during examinations. He remembered at the induction evening that the police lead trainer and the course leader at the university had discussed the possibility of a dyslexia assessment if anyone in the cohort had any concerns. He contacted his course leader at the university and a dyslexia assessment was booked in for him the following week.
>
> The dyslexia assessment consisted of a series of tests to assess Peter in areas such as reading, writing and spelling. The assessment also included areas such as speed of processing and memory and fine motor skills. A few days after the test, Peter received a written report detailing the results of his dyslexia assessment, which confirmed a diagnosis of dyslexia. The report detailed which areas Peter would require some support in and detailed some recommendations to help him while studying and in the workplace. It was recommended that he would be offered extra support with his written work, extra time in exams and extensions on his written submissions at university if required.

Conclusion

During your apprenticeship it is important that you work collaboratively with your employer and training provider to successfully complete it. There is a wealth of support and expertise available to assist and guide you through every aspect of your programme, whether when on operational duty or at university. To successfully complete your apprenticeship, all parties in the PCDA triangle must work together to ensure that you have the support and opportunities to guide you through the process. You have a significant part to play as well by ensuring that you complete your force operational competencies and successfully complete your academic programme to the best of your ability. It is very important that you utilise the support available to you to achieve your grade aspirations and attend all your scheduled tripartite meetings for bespoke support and guidance throughout your apprenticeship.

Further reading

Importance of teamwork in the police

College of Policing (2022) *We Are Collaborative*. [online] Available at: https://profdev.college.police.uk/competency-values/we-are-collaborative (accessed 27 November 2022).

Smart targets and target setting

Life Hack (2022) *What Is Goal Setting and How It Leads to a Fulfilling Life*. [online] Available at: www.lifehack.org/articles/lifestyle/goal-setting-the-why-behind-the-what.html (accessed 27 November 2022).

Key links for support

ADHD Foundation – www.adhdfoundation.org.uk

British Dyslexia Association – www.bdadyslexia.org.uk

Dyspraxia Foundation – https://dyspraxiafoundation.org.uk

National Autism Society – www.autism.org.uk

4 Getting prepared for your EPA gateway

LEARNING OBJECTIVES

After reading this chapter you will be able to:

- understand the importance of planning for your gateway point in Year 3;
- explain the milestones in each year of the PCDA programme which must be achieved to progress to the next stage;
- critically review the evidence-based research project submission criteria and produce a plan to achieve these requirements.

Introduction

This chapter introduces you to the gateway of the PCDA that occurs in Year 3 of your apprenticeship, equipping you with the knowledge required to achieve the key milestones in each year of the PCDA programme. This will ensure that the knowledge and skills required to move forward to the next stage of the apprenticeship are achieved. This chapter also details assessment 2 of the EPA, the evidence-based research project (EBRP), which is an independent research project that you will complete in an area of operational policing in Year 3.

As stated previously in the book, it is very important that you prepare for the EPA from the start of your apprenticeship. Specific milestones must be successfully achieved in order to progress to the next stage in the programme. These are broken down and discussed below.

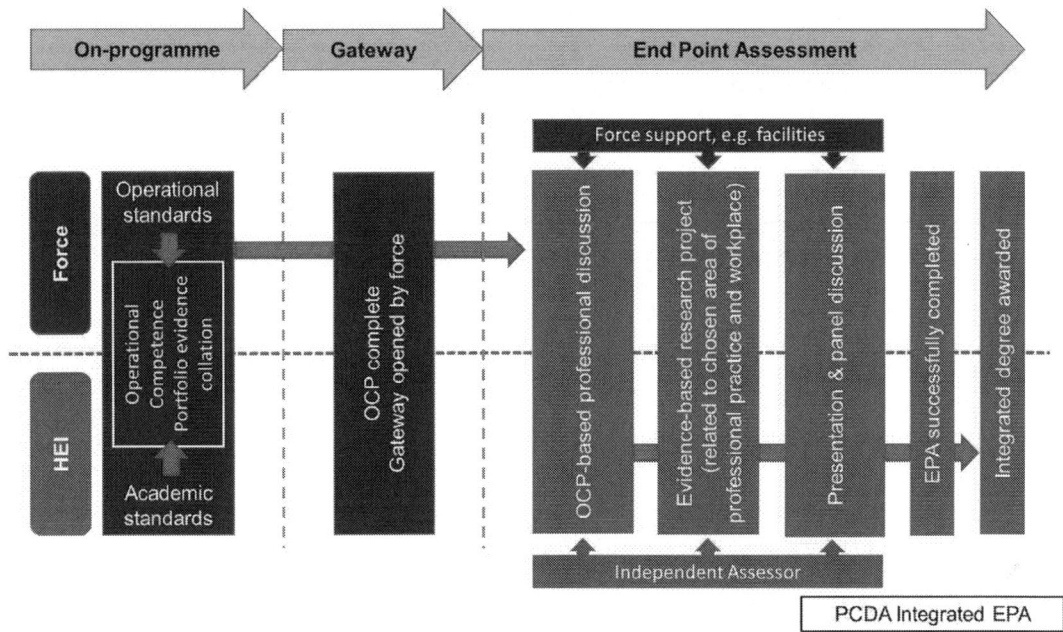

Figure 4.1 *Flow chart detailing progression through the PCDA programme (IfATE, 2017)*

Key milestones throughout the PCDA programme

Year 1, level 4

Year 1 is often called the settling-in year as it can sometimes be quite a step up from level 3 learning at college or sixth form to level 4 at university. During the first academic year of your programme at university, you will be taught the basics of academic skills and writing to assist you with your submissions for your modules at university. You will also learn new skills and theory with your police trainers, which will be assessed by the police. You will gather evidence of your operational competencies in the form of a portfolio. This will either be in the form of an e-portfolio (where you upload your evidence logs onto an online platform) or in paper format.

You will start collating evidence for this portfolio very early on in your programme when you are on duty on your work-based placements with the police. Working with the police, you will ensure that the Operational Competence Portfolio (OCP, a portfolio of evidence for operational competency) is collated and key milestones are met in the recommended timescales. The completion of the OCP is a gateway requirement.

Evidence for your portfolio will be collated during months 1–24 (typically) to populate the OCP. The standards of competency defined within the OCP (relating to distinct operational duties) will be set and maintained by the professional body (College of Policing) and contribute to consistency and standardisation on a national basis (IfATE, 2017). The OCP will include the minimum standard for Independent Patrol Status (IPS). This is the standard by which the apprentice is deemed to have safely and lawfully evidenced sufficient competency to operate as a police constable in the workplace, but not the achievement of full competency – completion of the EPA will determine full competency. IPS should be complete and achieved by the end of Year 1.

Preparing for your professional discussion element of the EPA from day one

Your portfolio of evidence will be used by the Independent Assessor (IA) to assess your first component of the end-point assessment (EPA), the professional discussion. The IA, following the review of the OCP, will assess the application of all core workplace-based policing (KSBs). When you start to populate your portfolio with evidence logs it is useful to be mindful from day one that the IA will need to read through your portfolio to prepare questions for your professional discussion.

Top tips for your portfolio

- All submitted evidence logs must be clearly labelled and referenced, for example, Evidence 1 (only use this reference once).
- It most likely will be split into two parts – evidence for your IPS submissions and sign-off by your tutor, and your Full Operational Competence (FOC) submissions and sign-off by your work-based assessor.
- Ensure the text boxes in the evidence log document contain adequate detail for the IA to read and fully understand the type of incident that you attended and what happened before, during and after the incident.
- Ensure that what operational competencies that you are claiming are clearly detailed on the evidence log in your portfolio.
- A clear and detailed self-reflection with regard to the incident should be included in the evidence log. What went well? What not so well? How will you improve your professional practice when you deal with a similar incident in the future?
- Ensure that the document is spell checked and neatly written/typed out, is accessible and easy to read. The IA, the person conducting your mock EPA and work-based police assessor have to read the documents in your portfolio.
- You will have to revise each document in your portfolio for your EPA; ensure that it has clear prompt points in the evidence log so that you can remember clearly what occurred at the incident.
- Revise regularly and you will be able to answer questions regarding your portfolio with ease and confidence during your EPA.

TASK

- Review your portfolio and identify any gaps in each of the evidence logs in your portfolio.
- Are all documents clearly labelled on the uploaded or paper-based document?
- Are the evidence logs clear and easy to read for you and the IA?
- Spend time making a plan to rectify any gaps and complete it as soon as possible.

Year 1 review

By the end of Year 1, you must have completed and achieved the following to progress to Year 2.

1. Off-the-job training (OTJT) tracker is complete for Year 1 and you have attended all tripartite reviews and achieved targets set in meetings.
2. All academic assignments and tasks are complete and achieved. Any module resits for failed elements are complete and achieved.
3. IPS is achieved and signed off as complete by the police.
4. FOC portfolio is on track and you have hit targets set.
5. Maths/English on track/completed if required to be taken.

Year 2, level 5 will be very similar to Year 1, where you will be taught in protected learning blocks at university which will be delivered by both university academic staff and police trainers. You will now go into more specific detail in the core policing areas and maybe starting to consider if you would like to specialise in a particular area of policing. In Year 2 you will be asked to start to consider any areas or issues in policing that you would like to research for your EBRP, which you will complete in Year 3.

Year 2 review

By the end of Year 2, you must have completed and achieved the following to progress to Year 3.

1. All academic assignments and tasks complete and achieved.
2. FOC complete and signed off.
3. OTJT tracker complete for Year 2; targets met and achieved.
4. Maths/English on track or achieved.

Year 3, level 6

It is very important that all assignments, trackers and your FOC are complete and achieved before moving into Year 3. Sometimes if you have failed to achieve an element of an assessment or a couple of your FOCs you may be able to complete the outstanding work a couple of weeks into Year 3. Your target will be set that you complete all assessment criteria for Year 2 by the end of the academic year. In Year 3, you will have your level 6 modules to complete and will be required to plan for your EPA near to the end of Year 3, so it is important that you are not carrying over work from Year 2 into Year 3. Before you can be considered for the gateway and ready for your EPA you must complete certain criteria before progression takes place.

What is the gateway?

The gateway takes place before your EPA can start. The employer (police) and the training provider (university) will review your KSBs to see if you have met the minimum requirements of the apprenticeship set out in the PC apprenticeship standard. They will decide, based on your progress, if you are ready to take the final assessment (ESFA, 2022b). If you are not fully ready to take your EPA, a bespoke plan will be implemented to ensure that you are EPA ready as soon as practicable. The gateway occurs in Year 3; you will be given detail of a designated gateway week when you undergo your induction in Year 3. This detail can also be found in your course and module handbook online.

Minimum requirements

To meet the minimum requirements set out in the apprenticeship standard you will need to successfully complete or do the following.

- Display occupational competency (completion of your FOC).
- Have evidence of or pass functional skill levels in English and maths.
- Complete mandatory training such as personal safety training and first aid.
- Take any qualifications set out in the standard (on track to complete your academic programme).
- Meet the minimum duration for their apprenticeship training.

Only PCDA apprentices who complete the gateway successfully can start the EPA (ESFA, 2022b).

Resits and retakes of the EPA

You will not be able to complete your apprenticeship without fully achieving all components of the EPA. If you fail to successfully achieve one or more of the components of the EPA, you will be offered the opportunity to resit that element again. This is permitted in line with the higher education regulator's requirements and the requirements of Police Regulations, including timescales. To aid national consistency, no more than three resits/retakes per element will be permitted. If you do fail any of the EPA elements (including the EBRP), you will be offered bespoke help and support to ensure that you are ready to retake your assessment again.

A resit cannot be taken with the intention of increasing the original grade if you have passed your EPA. Resits are only to be taken in the event of failure. It is very important that no apprentice should progress through the gateway and take their EPA if they are not ready to take their final assessment.

What is an EBRP?

Assessment component 1, the professional discussion, and assessment component 3, the presentation and panel discussion, are discussed in detail in Chapter 6. This chapter looks at the EPA component 2, the EBRP.

The College of Policing (2022d) outlines evidence-based policing as an approach where officers review and use the best available evidence to inform and challenge policies, practices and decisions. The 'best available evidence' involves using appropriate research methods and sources for the questions being asked. Research should be carefully conducted, with transparency about its methods, limitations and how its conclusions were reached. The theoretical basis and context of the research should be made clear. Research can be used to:

- develop a better understanding of an issue – by describing the nature, extent and possible causes of a problem or looking at how a change was implemented;
- assess the effect of a policing intervention – by testing the impact of a new initiative in a specific context or exploring the possible consequences of a change in policing.

Evidence-based policing does not provide definitive answers that officers and staff should apply uncritically. Officers and staff will reflect on their practice, consider how the 'best available' evidence applies to their day-to-day work, and learn from their successes and failures. The approach should mean that officers and staff can ask questions, challenge accepted practices and innovate in the public interest. The research project has a practical policing purpose: demonstrating learning, critical thinking and problem-solving skills.

PCDA apprentices are encouraged to adopt the philosophy of evidence-based policing to question the sources of evidence, their reliability, validity and the possible presence of bias. The benefits of adopting such a philosophy are many and varied, but include the development of the evidence base for establishing the profession of policing and the identification of innovative solutions by practitioner-researchers who have an insight into workplace needs that can be shared across the police service. The development of individual practitioner skills empowers self-actualising police officers by exposing the expertise within academic higher education partnerships directly to the realities of contemporary policing.

Overview of the EBRP

Assessment 2 of the EPA requires you to conduct an independent piece of research into an area of policing using appropriate research methodologies and techniques. The research will be written up in the form of a 10,000-word project (or equivalent). The subject matter of the EBRP should be agreed in partnership with the police, higher education institution and apprentice in advance of the project commencing to ensure it has potential to add value to the organisation. The EBRP has a pass mark of 50 per cent.

How is it taught?

You will be supported to undertake your EBRP through a combination of taught workshops, individual supervision by your academic supervisor and by the module leader. You may also have a designated specialist point of contact in your force who can assist you with your research (if applicable).

Academic support and supervision

Throughout the module, you will have regular contact with the module leader and police trainers through the scheduled taught sessions and a series of drop-ins/meetings. If you have any specific learning needs, please discuss these with your module leader at the earliest opportunity.

In addition, you will be allocated an academic supervisor. Where possible, academic supervisors are allocated based on their area of expertise. The role of the academic supervisor is to guide you through the research process and the process of completing a research project. The role of the academic supervisor is to facilitate discussion about the EBRP and to make general points about proposed topic areas and methodology when appropriate. Discussion will focus upon the process and timeline of the EBRP, on preparation, research areas, note taking and writing. In addition, issues surrounding presentation, referencing and writing style can be supported by library staff. Details of how to book an appointment can be found on your VLE site or by contacting the law/policing librarian at your respective university. They will not specifically advise how to conduct your research or how to write your research project; this is an independent piece of research completed by you.

You will be informed of your academic supervision hours during the module induction, and information on this can be found in the EBRP module handbook on your VLE. If you are unsure of this information, contact your module leader. When you meet with your supervisor (this can be online or face to face), this time will be used to discuss your project, to look at draft chapters and to give general advice. The typical amount of time designated for supervision purposes varies nationally, but is usually between five to eight hours for each student. Consider when you will require the most support – at the beginning? When formulating your research question? Recommendations and conclusion?

Plan your time wisely as your supervisor will be keeping a log of the time allocation and when it has been used.

Supervisor–student relationships are very important during the supervision process. Contact at regular intervals is important; do not try to cram lots of meetings in at the end. Ensure that you plan your meetings with your supervisor; bring an agenda and have specific items/questions to discuss. You must contact your supervisor in advance to book appointments, so you have a clear plan of completing your project. Your supervisor can guide and support you but they are unable to tell you what to do with your project, such as a research question or topic, or mark your work and give you a grade for what they have seen. Normally, draft chapters must be submitted to a supervisor no later than two weeks before the end of supervision. You must complete the last two weeks before submission working independently without supervisor support.

Supervisor–student expectations

To ensure that the staff–student supervision relationship between staff and student is successful, it is important to have some expectations and boundaries in place.

Staff expectations

Staff expectations of students include:

- being proactive in initiating contact with the supervisor as necessary;
- making regular appointments for supervision sessions;
- attending the meeting with an agenda with planned questions and discussion;
- taking responsibility for their EBRP and plan work and milestones;
- working towards meeting jointly agreed targets throughout the process;
- submitting draft work in advance of meetings. Students must be mindful that supervisors will be teaching in the week and give adequate time to respond after reading your work. Staff will normally read each chapter or piece of information once only.

Student expectations

Student expectations of academic supervision include:

- supporting students in planning and carrying out their research project;
- being available for appointments and be responsive to emails;
- offering suggestions, ideas and advice in response to students' reading, writing and research;
- reading draft work submitted in advance of a meeting;
- providing constructive feedback on content and structure of draft work in a timely manner;
- assisting them in developing a plan for targets and key milestones.

Starting your EBRP

Each university will typically have a different method of delivery and it is important to attend sessions and read the available information on your VLE site. When your research topic is identified, it is important that you start to read around your subject area and start to gather information which may be beneficial to your research.

The research proposal and ethics application must be completed, submitted and gain approval prior to any research taking place. This will be discussed in detail in your teaching sessions before submission takes place. Planning and preparation are key; work with your supervisor to produce a workable and achievable project timeline.

Available literature in your topic area

During your first meeting with your supervisor, there will be an expectation that you will be able to demonstrate some initial familiarity with the literature relevant to the topic under consideration. Reviewing articles in journals or textbooks is a useful starting point. Book a session with library staff who will be able to locate and source relevant information and can offer workshops regarding sourcing material for your project. Your EBRP should have a robust academic foundation and a wide range of sources is expected in your project. You must also demonstrate a high level of engagement of sources that use academic writing.

While useful, you need to be mindful of the sources that you use when researching and writing your project. You must use reliable and academically sound information and be cautious while using online internet sources. It is not recommended that you rely on websites such as Wikipedia, which may be unreliable sources; all resources must be fully and correctly referenced.

Types of evidence-based research projects

All EBRPs must have a significant research element and involve an action research approach. Your EBRP will be focused on a specialist area or topic of operational activity in the police. Each police–higher education institution collaboration will have their own agreed policy for the EBRP and you must refer to your own university for actual and specific guidance for your research project. It is generally commonplace that your research topic will be required to be jointly agreed between you, your police force and the university. They must also involve some type of data collection and analysis. There are two key types of data.

1. **Primary data** – a type of data that is collected directly by a researcher from first-hand sources, using methods such as surveys, interviews or focus groups.
2. **Secondary data** – data gathered from studies, surveys and interviews which have been conducted by other people or research.

All EBRPs, regardless of the types of data collected and engaged with, are a sound research base and are of equal merit; you will not be penalised for using one set of data. Depending on your approach to data collection and analysis for your research, your EBRP will be either primary-research based or secondary-research based. It is very important that you carefully consider which type of data you are going to engage with before starting your research.

Methodological considerations

- What people or organisations will data be collected from?
- How should data be collected?
- How should data be analysed?
- How do I seek access to respondents?
- What are the key problems encountered in undertaking research?
- How can I ensure that I conduct ethical research?

TASK

Primary or secondary data considerations

- How will data be used in your research project and how will it enable you to respond to your research question?
- Is your data collection approach feasible given the time and resources available to you?
- What ethical issues are associated with your chosen approach and method of data collection?
- Would it be realistic to expect in-depth interviews with police officers in your topic area? Would they be honest in their answers if the questions posed were very contentious? What implications would this have?
- How would you deal with apathy from police officers in specialist areas of policing who receive large numbers of questionnaires to complete from student officers?

Limitations of your data collection

During your presentation and panel interview, you will be expected to discuss the limitations of your research and you should prepare for this when writing up your findings. You should emphasise that your data is illustrative. For example, one focus group could have particularly negative views about a subject area but is not representative of the whole force or policing area. Only using a small sample size can sometimes have a detrimental effect on the research outcomes. Some officers may be hesitant to give their honest view in some questioning even though the questions are asked anonymously. A common question asked by the panel to students after their presentation is to consider whether they would do anything differently if they started their research today. For further details regarding panel questions please refer to Chapter 6.

Research data scrutiny

Claims from research data and statistics often seem very convincing. When used appropriately, they add credence to an argument. However, it has been said that statistics can be used to prove anything. Where scientific reports tend to be painstakingly exact in their claims and detail, beware of writers using research data in vague terms. Always check the reliability of your sources and information (Hills, 2011).

Questions to ask about research data and statistics

- What claim is being made from the data?
- Is the result what you would have reasonably expected?
- How exact is their claim? Examine the statistics. Words like 'majority' require further examination: was the majority 51 per cent or 99 per cent?
- Check the date of the research data. Are the results still relevant and current? Or have they been superseded by subsequent research?
- Where was the data published? Is this a trusted source?
- An important consideration for research data is how was the research funded? Check that there are no vested interests, such as research into the benefits of using a taser being funded by a taser manufacturer.
- How big is the sample size? A small sample is less statistically significant and could be deemed unreliable. A bigger sample is easier to generalise from.

Ethical considerations and standards

Research ethics are the set of ethics that govern how scientific and other research is performed at research institutions such as universities, and how it is disseminated. Each university will have its own bespoke policy and it is important that you read the guidance carefully before submitting your ethics proposal for scrutiny by the ethics panel at your university. There will be detailed advice regarding ethics on your university website and also the module VLE. This will also be covered in the teaching sessions of your EBRP module. If you have any queries, contact your module leader who will be able to assist you.

Principles of good ethical research include the following.

- It demonstrates that you agree to the accepted ethical standards of a genuine research study.
- The research is honest, rigorous, transparent and respectful.

- Participants are informed about who has access to their data and how it will be used.
- Participation is voluntary and informed, free from coercion or undue influence.
- The research can be defined as worthwhile and proves value that outweighs any harm.

Assessment criteria

Comprehensive and specific detail regarding the structure and assessment requirements for your EBRP can be found in the your university's module handbook. As with all other modules that you have studied on your programme, each assessment will have its own learning objectives that you must achieve and they will be found in your assignment brief.

Through your EBRP you are expected to demonstrate the following:

- a critical evaluation of a complex body of policing-related knowledge;
- application of appropriate research methodologies and techniques;
- analytical techniques and problem-solving skills applied in a policing context;
- the ability to gather and analyse relevant material to inform judgements that include critical reflection on relevant social or ethical issues;
- effective presentation of information, ideas, problems and solutions to both specialist and non-specialist audiences;
- comprehensive understanding of the potential impact of recommendations on the workplace, workforce and service;
- qualities and skills necessary to continue to undertake further development with a high degree of autonomy.

TASK

Read the assessment guidance for the EBRP module.

- What are the requirements? Is it one piece of written work or is it composed of different tasks?
- Produce a timeline of the key milestones for this module and how you will achieve the assessment requirements.

If you are unsure of the topic area allocated, find a suitable contact within that policing area and request a meeting to gain further insight into that policing area.

EBRP grading

Table 4.1 EBRP grading template

Grade	Grading description
Distinction (70% and over)	The student has met all the learning outcomes of the assessment with evidence of comprehensive and up-to-date knowledge and understanding of concepts and theories and their interrelationship. The work shows a detailed appreciation of how aspects of the subject are uncertain, contradictory or limited. The student's work has a well-sustained approach using a breadth of evidence, reasoning and reflection. Work shows evidence of a mature and independent approach to problem-solving. The student can create appropriate hypotheses and select, justify and use imaginative and innovative approaches in their investigations.
Pass (50–69%)	The student has met all the underpinning KSBs, with sound evidence of detailed knowledge and understanding of key concepts and theories, including interrelationships, and an awareness of how aspects of the subject are uncertain, contradictory or limited. The work adopts a critical approach using a breadth of evidence, reasoning and reflection. The work shows evidence that the student can act autonomously in the identification and definition of complex problems and select, justify and use approaches aimed at their resolution.
Fail (0–49%)	The student has not met all the underpinning KSBs, with only a basic knowledge of key concepts and theories and weaknesses in understanding. There is little or no recognition of the complexity of the subject. The work is largely descriptive and has insufficient or inappropriate evidence to substantiate assertions. Analysis is minimal or contradictory. Unable to always apply learning accurately to complex problems and/or practical contexts. Work which contains evidence of, or reference to, unlawful, unsafe or dangerous practice should be deemed a fail.

Criticality

To obtain higher grading in your EBRP and other assessments such as essays and reports, you must master critical thinking and analysis in your work.

A common sentence in feedback on submitted work from university tutors is that students do not think critically enough. Essays are '*too descriptive*', '*have no evidence*' or '*show no argument*'. However, while students are expected to think critically and assessments are graded on this ability, a critical approach is rarely explained (Hills, 2011).

A critical approach applies to all university study and your time in operational policing: not only reading and writing assignments and police statements, but listening in lectures, giving presentations and speaking in seminars.

A critical approach involves a number of skills, including:

- precision both in understanding academic texts and in writing your own;
- being able to form and to follow arguments;

- logical reasoned thinking;
- knowing when to take information at face valve and when to challenge it;
- analysing and evaluating information;
- understanding issues from perspectives other than your own;
- selecting the right knowledge for the task posed.

You are required to think critically because it is part of your learning journey at university; there are always different schools of thought and views on almost everything. Every assessment, from coursework to exams, is marked according to an agreed set of standards – the assessment criteria. Each module that you will study on the PCDA programme will have learning outcomes (LOs) that you must achieve to successfully complete and pass that module. You will find this information in your module handbook and assessment brief for each module that you study. It is important that you understand the assessment criteria before you start your coursework, otherwise you might not fully answer the question(s) posed.

The PCDA has an assessment criteria template (or rubric) that your lecturer will refer to when they mark and grade your work for each assessment. To achieve a higher grade, the work will include some of the following common examples (all will require critical thinking skills):

- demonstrates an ability to think critically;
- good depth of analysis;
- strong arguments put forward;
- identifies key debates;
- evidence of independent thinking;
- large range of sources used in their work;
- good evaluation of source material.

The following assessment criteria will be used to award lower scores (lack of critical thinking):

- weak, structured answer;
- no argument;
- overly descriptive;
- has not answered the question posed;
- inappropriate/irrelevant material;
- limited reasoning;
- opinions expressed without evidence.

Thinking and writing critically is imperative to you achieving those higher grades that you aspire to obtain. You will learn methods in research skills sessions and don't forget to book a study skills session with staff in your library who will be happy to assist you. You will also find lots of tips and guidance on your university library website, which you can access from home or at work.

Taking a critical approach to writing: differences between descriptive and critical writing

Table 4.2 The distinct difference between descriptive and critical writing

Descriptive writing	Critical writing
Describes a process such as a stop search of a person.	Shows the strengths and weaknesses of this process or suggests a better alternative.
States what a theory is, such as why people commit crime.	Evaluates this theory by examining its argument.
States what other academics have said.	Makes a convincing argument in answer to a specific question.
Lists information, ideas and details regarding a specific topic.	Relates these ideas to the question; evaluates the importance of each after scrutiny, shows links, parallels and contrasts in the information.

Stages involved in critical thinking

There are stages involved in critical thinking which start simply and then progress to more complex. Each stage needs to be completed before moving to the next stage. If you have not completed a scoping exercise regarding the proposed content of your work, completed some reading or attended your university lectures, you will not have the knowledge to move to the next stage of critical thinking.

Stage 1: Knowledge

This is the first stage when you encounter something new for the first time, for example a new law or policing policy. Your knowledge is shown by the ability to recall, repeat, memorise and reproduce. But being able to quote the police caution or list the order when writing a police statement does not necessarily mean that you understand the information.

Stage 2: Comprehension

Until you understand something, you cannot scrutinise it critically. In your EBRP writing (or any written piece of work), the ability to effectively paraphrase (put a writer's ideas in your own words) shows that you comprehend what you have read. When at university you need to use your knowledge and demonstrate this in a range of assessments.

Stage 3: Application

Here, you show you can apply theories and arguments. In vocational subjects such as policing, the ability to put theory into practice is crucial. Case studies, scenarios and problem-solving are common assignments which ask you to use your theoretical knowledge for a practical purpose. Applying knowledge shows it has a real purpose. However, you must consider your information carefully and should not apply it without question or scrutiny by accepting it at face value. This is not an issue with uncontested knowledge such as accepted facts and widely used principles. However, contested knowledge should never be accepted at face value; careful analysis is required.

Stage 4: Analysis

Analysis involves examining ideas carefully, breaking them down and questioning them closely. Seeing patterns in data, understanding how parts of a system are organised and reading between the lines are all part of analysis. This is a key aspect of critical thinking. Questions that ask you to compare and contrast, to explain why or to examine an argument are asking for you to analyse the information. During your literature review for your EBRP, you will read lots of literature in relation to your research area with lots of differing views. You will be required to analyse the main theoretical positions and central arguments in the literature that you read.

Stage 5: Synthesis

Synthesis means bringing together all the information that you have researched. Throughout your reading, you will have selected relevant information, noted recurrent themes and noticed how ideas from different sources link. The more you read in your field of research, the wider the pool of knowledge you will be able to draw from.

Stage 6: Evaluation

Evaluation is the highest level of critical thinking and is crucial to obtain the higher grades that you aspire to on your programme. When you evaluate the information you have read, you need to consider the following – what are the competing arguments and contradictory theories in this area?

To evaluate:

- know and understand the information you have read;
- analyse the text carefully;
- consider the text in relation to others that you have read and relate them to your question.

Table 4.3 Critical thinking assignment recap (Hills, 2011)

✓ Yes	✗ No
Read as widely as you can, especially for coursework assignments and your research project.	Describe in too much detail unless specifically asked. You need to carefully select what needs to be explained or described before moving on to analysis.
Look at assignment questions carefully to work out what type of thinking is required.	Forget that in order to evaluate well, you will need to be able to understand, apply, analyse and synthesise – there is no shortcut.
Think about the texts you have read. Are you applying? Analysing? Evaluating?	Memorise without understanding – you will never get past stage 1.

CASE STUDIES

Peter

In Chapter 3, Peter discovered that he was dyslexic after undergoing a dyslexic assessment. He was struggling to concentrate in his learning sessions in the classroom and online. He was sent his dyslexia report and recommendations after his assessment, which he forwarded to the police and the university, and a learning support plan (or learning contract) was put in place. The recommendations to support Peter were implemented at university and in the workplace to ensure that Peter was not at any disadvantage to his colleagues with regard to his dyslexia diagnosis.

Peter was particularly nervous about the EBRP module and the completion of a 10,000-word research project. He was feeling very anxious about the process and in the first teaching session for this module he asked to see the lecturer after the session for some reassurance. The module leader was aware of the learning contract in place and the support that was recommended to assist Peter with all his assignment submissions. A bespoke support plan was implemented for Peter and he was offered ten hours' support with a learning support tutor, who proofread and helped with his grammar and sentence construction. Peter also had lots of support from his EBRP supervisor, who supported him with his research and construction of his research project. He also attended workshops in the study skills centre in the library. Overall, Peter felt very supported and really enjoyed researching his topic. He worked very hard and achieved 68 per cent for his research project, which he was delighted to be awarded. He was very grateful for all the support and guidance that he received and now is a mentor for other students with dyslexia and other learning disabilities with the police.

> **Rosie**
>
> Rosie had issues with her time management during her apprenticeship and had a tendency to leave all her written submissions at university until the last minute and submit just before the deadline. As the EBRP is a piece of largely independent study, Rosie did not contact her supervisor or module leader to arrange meetings to support her through the research project process. After many failed communication attempts by telephone and email, no staff were able to contact Rosie and assist her with her EBRP. Rosie contacted her supervisor two days before the submission deadline and failed to submit her work on the deadline and as a consequence failed her EBRP module. Due to failing this module, which is a component of the EPA, she was unable to undertake her EPA until the EBRP was resubmitted and achieved. Rosie had to be back coursed to a later cohort and did not eventually complete and pass her EPA until five months later. Her employing police force were not happy with the delay to her being confirmed in post and she is now on a development plan with the police.

Conclusion

Planning and preparation are key to successful completion of your apprenticeship programme. Using foresight to plan assessments and milestones at the start of each academic year will ensure success during your academic studies and operationally with the police. The gateway is a major milestone in your apprenticeship programme; when you successfully pass through the gateway you are ready to undertake the final assessment of the PCDA, the EPA. The EPA is comprised of three elements, all of which must be successfully achieved to pass the EPA. This chapter has covered the EBRP, which is part of your EPA, and detailed the importance of working closely with your supervisor to ensure success in this element of the EPA.

Further reading

Bullock, K, Fielding, N and Holdaway, S (2019) *Critical Reflections on Evidence-based Policing*. London: Routledge.

Burns, T and Sinsfield, S (2016) *Essential Study Skills: The Complete Guide to Success at University*. 4th ed. London: Sage.

Hart, C (1998) *Doing a Literature Review: Releasing the Social Science Imagination*. London: Sage.

5 Understanding, planning and preparing for your assessments

> **LEARNING OBJECTIVES**
>
> After reading this chapter you will be able to:
>
> - identify key people involved in your end-point assessment;
> - understand the components of the end-point assessment;
> - explain the importance of the planning and preparation required to be successful in your end-point assessment;
> - critically reflect on your own strengths and areas for development to ensure success in your final assessment.

Introduction

Planning and preparation are key to successfully getting ready for any assessment. This chapter covers the importance of planning for your end-point assessment (EPA) from the start of your apprenticeship. Throughout the PCDA, you will be assessed both by the police, who will access your occupational competencies when on duty, and by your university, where you will need to successfully complete all modules on your programme to progress. This chapter introduces you to the key people involved in the EPA process and the importance of preparing for both the mock EPA as well as the final assessment near to the end of your programme.

Key people involved in the PCDA EPA

Independent Assessors

Independent Assessors (IAs) will assess all elements of the EPA.

- They must be independent of the process with no involvement in the employment or training of the apprentice to ensure a robust and fair assessment process and are recruited by the university.
- All IAs must be occupationally knowledgeable in relation to the role of the police constable. They must have actively carried out the role, or trained officers for at least one year in the last three years, to carry out an EPA. This ensures that the IA is occupationally qualified and current in their policing practice knowledge to assess new police constables.
- They must have ongoing police and assessment related continuing professional development (CPD). They must also be professionally qualified as an assessor in line with policing and higher education sector requirements.
- The IA has final responsibility for assessment and grading decisions for all elements of the EPA (IfATE, 2017). The IA is given access to your work-based Operational Competence Portfolio (OCP) before your EPA so they can ask you specific questions related to incidents you have attended. They will also grade your research project that you have submitted to the university.

TASK

Roles and responsibilities of an assessor

- Research and list the roles and responsibilities of an assessor.
- Throughout your PCDA programme, who else will be assessing your work and occupational competencies?
- What are the policies specific to your force with regards to quality assurance?

A representative from your university

During the EPA process there will also be a representative from the university in attendance for one component of the EPA – the presentation and panel discussion. This may be your research project supervisor, your mentor/tutor or another member of staff from the university. They must also be occupationally knowledgeable in relation to the role of a police constable and have ongoing police-related CPD. They will ask you specific questions about your presentation and research project.

A representative from your police force (employer)

A representative from your police force will also be in attendance for the presentation and panel discussion element of the EPA. They will ask you questions regarding your research project outcomes and how your research findings can have a positive impact on policing both at local and national levels.

Overview of the key components of your end-point assessment

This EPA accompanies the PCDA Standard (this is discussed in detail in the next chapter). The EPA is the culmination of the apprenticeship and is undertaken near the end of the PCDA programme in Year 3. It is embedded within an integrated degree in Professional Policing Practice. Upon successful completion of the EPA, forces are responsible for the legal confirmation of apprentices in post. The EPA process has three distinct parts.

1. On programme

During your programme, you must successfully complete your work-based OCP, which covers all your operational competence requirements. This may be paper based or may be online in the form of an e-portfolio. When complete you will be 'signed off' as competent by your force before you are able to progress and move through the gateway. You must also successfully complete your programme of study at university before moving towards your final EPA.

2. Gateway

As previously discussed in Chapter 4, the gateway is when you successfully complete all the elements above. You may hear the term 'moving through the gateway', which means you have completed all requirements of your programme and are ready to undertake your final assessment – the EPA. The gateway week will vary depending on your university programme in Year 3 and you will be informed at the start of Year 3 when the gateway will occur. This will give you adequate time to plan for the gateway element of your programme.

3. The EPA

Table 5.1 Assessment components of the PCDA EPA

Assessment component	Task
1	Professional discussion between an Independent Assessor and the student officer following a review of the Operational Competence Portfolio (OCP).
2	Evidence-based research project (EBRP) – this will be marked and graded by university staff and the Independent Assessor.
3	Presentation regarding the methodology and findings of the EBRP followed by a panel discussion with representatives from the police and university, and the Independent Assessor.

The assessment components shown in Table 5.1 are graded against the assessment criteria, which are discussed in the next chapter. When all assessment components are complete and have been successfully achieved, the EPA is passed and the Integrated Degree is awarded. The apprentice is then confirmed in post as a substantive police officer.

What are coaching and mentoring?

From day one of the PCDA programme, you will have support and guidance from a range of staff, both from the police and your university. This will also apply to the EPA, where you will be given an opportunity for a mock EPA to coach and prepare you through the process. Coaching and mentoring are development approaches based on the use of one-to-one meetings or conversations to enhance an individual's skills, knowledge or work performance in their role. It is possible to draw distinctions between coaching and mentoring, although in the workplace the two terms may be used interchangeably (CIPD, 2022). Both are used regularly within the police service in training for student officers and experienced police officers who may be planning to enter a specialist role or for a promotion in police rank.

TASK

- What are the skills, qualities and behaviours you would expect a workplace coach or mentor to possess to successfully support and guide members of staff in the workplace?
- What would you consider to be the most important attributes?
- Why?

What is coaching?

The aim of coaching in the workplace is to produce optimal performance and improvement at work. Coaching focuses on specific skills and goals or areas where an individual requires additional support, such as social interaction, confidence, conflict management when on duty or presentation skills for a research assessment at university. The coaching process may last for a defined amount of time or could be ongoing until the student officer is confident to carry out that task and deemed to be competent in that area of work performance. Although there is much debate regarding precise definitions, coaching is generally approached in a similar way in most workplaces.

It is a skilled activity that should be delivered by people who are trained to coach, normally line managers such as sergeants, tutor constables or staff from the training department or outside organisation. Coaching focuses on improving performance and developing an individual at work. It provides people with the opportunity to better assess their strengths as well as their development areas through reflection both in the workplace and at university. When you are on probation this is commonplace. When undergoing work-based assessments and reflecting on your university assignments, you will be regularly tasked to reflect on your performance and conduct. During your mock EPA, you will have the opportunity to experience an EPA and will be asked questions and offered support and guidance on how to prepare for your final assessment.

What is mentoring?

Mentoring in the workplace is usually a process in which a more experienced colleague such as a tutor constable or a police officer with substantive service shares their knowledge to support the development of a new or less experienced member of staff. Mentoring calls on the skills of questioning, listening, clarifying and reframing that are also associated with coaching (CIPD, 2022). If you are a PCDA student officer, you will gain knowledge and theory in the classroom and will then apply this knowledge in practice when on your work placements, supported by an experienced police constable or a tutor constable. It can be quite daunting at first, but you must remember that all police officers have been in the same position as you and they too had to learn the craft of policing. It is their role to support and guide you on duty. An effective mentoring relationship is a learning opportunity for both participants, encouraging sharing and learning in the workplace and/or between roles.

Tutor constables

A tutor (including a tutor constable) provides mentoring, instruction and guidance as well as facilitating work-based learning, development and assessment on a one-to-one or small-group basis. Tutors plan for and enable work-based learning opportunities in a structured way, most typically using coaching, feedback and assessment skills (College of Policing, 2022e). When you start your first work-based placement or rotation after your learning block at university, you will be allocated a tutor constable, who will create a bespoke plan for you to demonstrate and achieve Full Operational Competence (FOC). This may be the same tutor constable throughout your programme for smaller police forces, but could change on each new work-based placement due to specialist skills and knowledge in that area of policing, for example, investigation. It is imperative that you start to gather evidence for your OCP and start to prepare for your EPA, even in the early stages of your programme.

Each learner is unique, and your learning journey may be very different to others in your cohort of student officers. We all have different learning styles and there are different coaching and mentoring models and theories available to assist new student officers. Coaching and mentoring in the workplace can enable individuals to meet personal, professional and organisational goals, for example to complete Independent Patrol Status (IPS) in Year 1 of the programme or to pass your EPA on your first attempt.

TASK

- Research different coaching and mentoring theories and models and consider how they can assist the development of new police officers to the service.
- If you were coaching or mentoring new or less experienced staff, what model/theories would you follow and why?
- How are they relevant in the context of policing and the police service?

Considerations when planning or participating in a coaching or mentoring session

Planning and preparation before the actual meeting by both the tutor/coach and the student officer are extremely important to ensure a successful and productive meeting takes place. Regular progress meetings for each student officer take place both with the employer (police force) and the training provider (university). It is very important a good professional relationship/rapport occurs from the first meeting to build trust and for the student officer to feel supported in this environment. When you have been allocated a mock EPA session, it is very important that you are prepared, have access to your portfolio to find evidence if required and are aware of the assessment criteria. It is recommended that you have a list of questions for the EPA coach to ask during your mock EPA to ensure that you understand the requirements of the forthcoming assessment.

These meetings will identify any issues or concerns and a bespoke plan will be put together to support the student officer both in the workplace and/or at the university. When arranging sessions, it is important to ensure that the room or place where the meeting will take place is suitable and offers privacy for the session. There should be no distractions, and the student officer will be at ease. During these sessions, the aim is to plan, prepare and facilitate learning opportunities, and to engage and support the student officer through their development process in order to meet designated learning outcomes and assessment criteria. An important aspect of review meetings with student officers is to help them to reflect on their work performance and provide them with feedback and monitoring of their progress, both in the workplace and their academic progress at university. Another important aspect of coaching/mentoring sessions is to support learners to build evidence of their progress and competence and develop bespoke action plans for their professional development. The tutor/coach should maintain records of meetings held and details of the learner's performance and development; this contributes to evidence of competence and, if required, supports formal performance procedures.

Work-based assessment within policing

As mentioned previously, PCDA student officers will undergo learning blocks of study at university and with the police, where they will be taught police theory and practice in the classroom and then put this knowledge into practice in the workplace. The student officer will be assessed in the workplace carrying out their role by their tutor and with some forces a team of work-based assessors will also assess them while on duty. This is to ensure that they have fully achieved their FOC, and they must complete an online learning portfolio. When the evidence is submitted to claim the required competencies, the evidence is then assessed by a force assessor who will deem it either sufficient or insufficient. If the evidence submitted fulfils the requirements, it will be signed off as complete. If it is not complete, a plan of action will be completed to assist the student officer in gaining meaningful evidence to be fully competent; or if this is difficult to obtain, a simulated scenario could be staged to enable the student to be assessed.

There are different types of assessment in the workplace. Formative assessment is designed to monitor student learning and provide ongoing feedback to students. It is an assessment for learning and if designed appropriately it can assist students to identify their strengths and weaknesses and obtain support for any area they are underachieving. Formative assessments can be tutor- or peer-led, or involve self-assessment and reflection. This type of assessment will not contribute to students' overall grade and can be considered as a practice assessment for their final assessments. Summative assessment is designed to evaluate student learning at the end of an instructional unit by comparing it against a standard or benchmark (University of Greenwich, 2022).

Reflective practice

The process used to learn from experience as an adult is described by Moon (1999) as reflection. Reflection with regard to your PCDA will involve looking back and evaluating incidents that you have attended in terms of what went well and what did not go so well, and how you could improve in the future if you had to deal with a similar incident or experience again. Reflective practice is a continual process throughout your apprenticeship and when used effectively can benefit you in many positive ways during your learner journey.

Learning from experience: the reflective learner

During your PCDA programme, you will spend time at university and with police trainers learning the key information and law required to effectively carry out your role as a police officer. You will then put that knowledge into practice when you undertake your work-based learning blocks on duty with the police. During this time, you will 'experience' operational policing. Kolb (1984) referred to this as the *experiential learning cycle*. Kolb described the ways that adults learn as a cycle of four stages that the learner goes through. He extended the idea that we learn from experience and suggested that we are able to do this by reflecting upon the things that have happened to us in order to make sense of them. Learning is therefore a process of experiences and reflections upon them.

The elements of the experiential learning cycle

Concrete experience

During our lives we may experience new or unfamiliar tasks or events. Kolb referred to these as concrete experiences. This could be a classroom experience, such as a new theory or legislation you have been learning at university. Alternatively, it may be an event that happened to you such as a driving lesson or making your first arrest.

Reflective observation

During and after the event, we reflect upon – in other words, think about – the experience that has taken place. This could be your first attempt at searching a member of the public or booking a detained person into custody. Reflective observation is the process of looking back on and remembering all the things that happened during the event.

Abstract conceptualisation

This refers to the process by which we start to make sense of the experience. We do this by thinking about the knowledge that we already have and reshaping it in order to include our experiences from the recent event. We can then form a new theory about the situation. By doing this we are able to learn new skills, ideas or pieces of knowledge; an example could be writing up a statement from a victim of crime.

Active experimentation

Once we have developed our new learning, we start to test it in other situations that we may encounter. The experimental stage is very important according to Kolb because it is only after we put our new ideas into practice that true learning has occurred.

TASK

Using Kolb's experiential cycle, think about a recent incident that you attended where you learnt something new. Then answer the following questions.

Describe what happened during the concrete experience.

- What did you attend?
- What was the reason for your attendance?
- What were your aims?
- Who else was involved in the event and what did they do?

→

> *Consider your reflections about this experience.*
> - What did you notice about attending this incident?
> - What were the differences and similarities during this incident that you have experienced before?
> - When dealing with this incident, what worked well for you and what did not work so well?
>
> *Assess your learning from attending this incident.*
> - What ideas and insights have you developed from this situation?
> - What skills did you use and have these developed from the start of your apprenticeship?
> - Are there any new skills that you need to learn?
>
> *Prepare to test your ideas in a new situation.*
> - Would your knowledge be useful in other situations?
> - Which skills have you developed during the PCDA that would be useful in other situations?
> - What could you change about the way you did things so that there is an improvement next time?

Learning as a cycle

It is important to understand from Kolb's model that learning takes place as a continuous cycle. Consider again the final part of the learning process, which involves testing out new learning in practice. When you have completed this, it becomes another event that has taken place. In other words, the active experimentation becomes a new concrete experience. The adult learner can then reflect on it, consider what they have learnt and test it in practice. The learner therefore continues to complete the learning cycle repeatedly, meaning that learning is a continuous and ongoing process throughout life (Copley, 2011).

Therefore, the PCDA is an effective way to learn and put your new skills into practice after a learning block at university, under the supervision of your tutor constable who guides and supports you when on operational duty.

Defining reflection

Kolb considered the reflective element of the learning cycle to be the process of 'thinking about' things that have taken place. We will now consider the views of Dewey (1933);

although he wrote about reflection in the 1930s, his work continues to be used and referred to in current textbooks that describe reflective activity. Dewey is still regarded as one of the founding fathers of reflection.

Dewey also suggested that learning takes place through thinking about events. He defined reflective thinking as *'The kind of thinking that consists in turning a subject over in the mind and giving it serious thought'* (Moon, 1999, p 12). Moon (1999) refers to the writings of Dewey (1933) in order to understand the principles of reflection and reflective practice. In order to understand situations, we develop a series of ideas that we link together in order to arrive at a meaning for them. The main reason for this is in order to solve what Dewey referred to as *'perplexity'*, which describes the feeling of doubt or uncertainty when we encounter a particular situation that may be unfamiliar to us. It is the confusion that arises from being presented with new and difficult issues that provides the motivation for us to make sense of them. Reflection, therefore, is a way of solving problems so that we can continue to understand the world around us (Copley, 2011).

Using reflective practice

From the onset of your PCDA programme, you will be asked to reflect regularly on your progress as an operational police officer and as a student at university. At university you may have to complete a reflective diary after your learning sessions and upload this onto the VLE that can be shared with your tutor. You may also keep a journal on your learner journey, reflecting on what has gone well, identifying areas of difficulty and formulating a plan to remedy the shortfall in your knowledge. When on operational duty and gathering evidence for your OCP, you will reflect on the incident that you attended and will reflect on your progress and how you dealt with that incident. You will make a short note on how you could improve the next time you deal with a similar incident to improve your performance. See Table 5.2 for an example of a reflection from a student officer after interviewing a suspect for a racially aggravated offence.

Table 5.2 Example of a reflective log from an OCP

Skills practised	Liaising with partner agencies Interviewing witnesses and victims Arranging solicitors Statement taking
Personal reflections	*This is the first time I have interviewed for racially aggravated public order so I planned well and took advice on whether the matter would be CPS or not. I had to learn the legislation for this matter, which made me understand the difference in sections of the legislation as to whether it would be CPS or not. The matter I interviewed for was section 5, which is a police charge, so this was new learning.* *Even though the outcome was conditional caution as the suspect was eligible, it was still a good job to investigate and there is prospect to charge should the caution not be abided by.*

	I feel moving forward I know and understand racially aggravated offences more now, which will benefit me when investigating in the future. I need to go over the legislation again and ensure that I fully understand all the law before I deal with a similar situation again.
Relevant prior learning	Public order legislation at university Interviewing and statement taking with the police Out-of-court disposal methods with the police

Other models of reflection

Sparkes (2014) created the RAISE model of reflection as other methods of reflection such as Kolb (1984) could be deemed as being too simplistic for the academic practitioner. With the emphasis now for police officers to engage with academic literature and evidence-based policing to assist them with their operational role, the RAISE model seeks to fill the gap. The model is easy to follow and encourages the operational practitioner to engage with theory and literature to improve their practice.

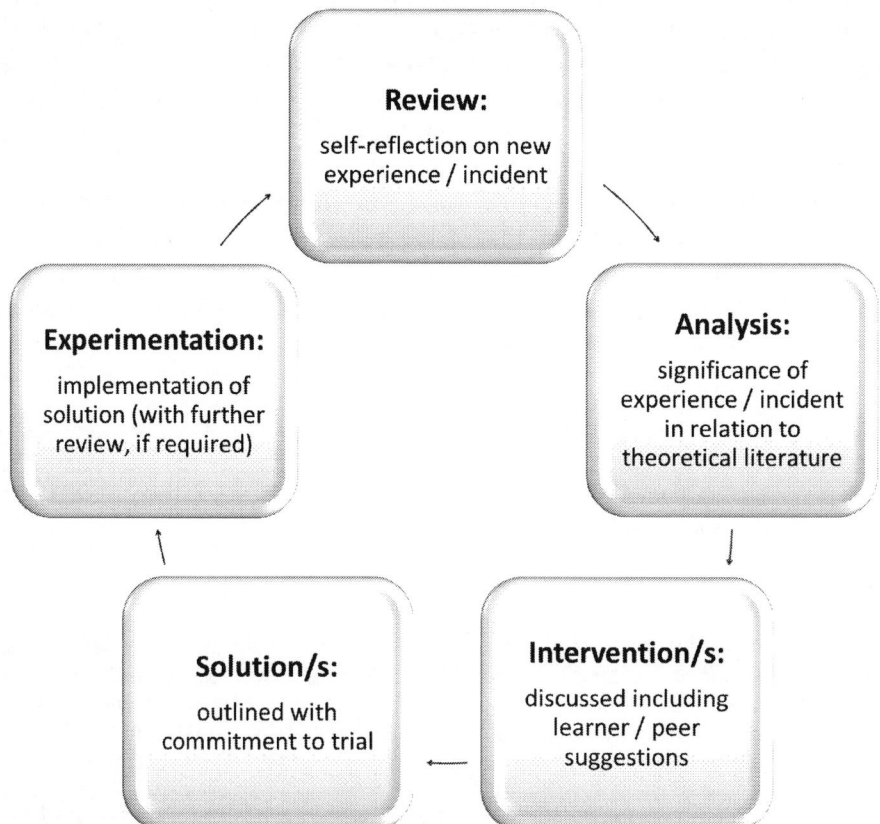

Figure 5.1 *RAISE model for policing practitioners*
(Sparkes, 2014)

We now move on to preparing for your mock EPA. Many students do not fully prepare for their mock EPA as they think that it is not important and so turn up totally unprepared for the session. The mock EPA is designed to prepare you for your final EPA. It is important that you have read through your portfolio and are ready to answer questions by the coach when prompted.

The mock EPA

The importance of planning and preparing for your mock and coaching session.

Essential tips

- Be fully prepared – read your portfolio of evidence before your mock EPA and think of more recent examples you have dealt with on duty in case they are needed in your assessment.
- Bring notes with you that detail examples of incidents that you have attended.
- Reflect on these incidents. What have you learnt? What did you do/would you improve next time?
- Ensure that you attend and use this time to assist you with your preparations for your final EPA. Use this time to ask your coach/mentor any questions that you may have about the forthcoming assessment.
- Make notes during the session and after it has concluded as prompts to assist you with preparing for your final EPA.

What will occur in your mock EPA session?

Your mock EPA will take place after you have successfully moved through the gateway. You will be allocated a practice session with a coach/mentor before the final EPA to ensure that you have adequate time to prepare and are ready to undertake your final assessment to conclude your apprenticeship. This may vary depending on the university you are attending and your employing police force. You will be notified in advance so that you can prepare for your mock assessment.

You should expect the following during your mock session EPA.

- Your coach/mentor for the mock session will introduce themselves and you will be asked to tell them your name and to show your ID before the session starts.
- They may ask you what your knowledge and understanding of the EPA process is currently to ascertain what support and guidance you may require.
- They will explain that the EPA process comprises three components – a professional discussion regarding your portfolio, your research project and a presentation and panel discussion. They may ask you to give an overview of your research project and its findings; be ready to discuss this with your coach.

- The EPA assessment criteria will be discussed with you, together with the importance of being knowledgeable of this before your actual assessment (this is be discussed in more detail in Chapter 6).

Questions will be open, such as: *Give me an example of a time when you used the National Decision Model (NDM) or when you searched a house.* Or specific questions will be asked relating to your evidence portfolio, for example: *Evidence 23 in your portfolio – you attended an address after reports of a vulnerable person who had been missing for over 24 hours. What was your plan of action to deal with this?*

You can use more recent examples of incidents you have dealt with but remember that your evidence in your portfolio has been internally verified by a police officer or a member of the assessment team at your force. They will have checked police systems that you have been involved in the assessment criteria that you are claiming. The IA will be assessing your portfolio but will be happy to listen to a recent example if it is strong and relevant and can be verified on police systems.

- You will be asked a range of questions relating to different criteria. Answer the question posed and be specific and concise with your answers. If you are unsure or do not understand the question, ask for clarification. You will have approximately five minutes to answer each question linked to the assessment criteria. Use this time wisely. If you do not attempt all questions, it will be an automatic failure of the EPA.
- After you have finished your answer, your coach will give you feedback about your answer and ask you to reflect on this – what could you do to improve? They will give you some support and guidance on how to improve your answer.

Because each EPA is bespoke to incidents that you personally have attended and dealt with, the coach will not be able to advise what you will be asked in your actual EPA. They can talk you through the assessment criteria and give you some examples of questions you may be asked. You must familarise yourself with the contents of your portfolio of evidence as some of the content could be a couple of years old. Your coach will check the timings of your answers and offer suggestions to improve for your final EPA.

After the mock session

- Make a plan of action for your final EPA. What went well? What needs further support? Critically reflect on how you performed in your mock EPA – how can you improve your answers?
- Make notes from the mock EPA to assist you with planning for the actual EPA. For the presentation, practise in front of a mirror or family and friends to build confidence in presenting information to a panel.
- Rehearse your timings – you will be given specific guidance for your presentation to ensure that you follow the assessment criteria. If you are instructed to only have ten slides in your presentation, follow these instructions carefully. If you do not follow instructions this will not be viewed favourably by the IA.

- If your EPA is being conducted online, practise sharing your presentation slides on Teams or Zoom before the actual assessment.
- A glass of water is a must as you will be talking a lot during the process.

Even though this is a mock assessment, your coach will run the session as if this is your final EPA. Ensure that you have your ID such as a passport or driving licence. Look smart, presentable and prepared for the session.

Remember: this session is available to you to offer support and guidance for the EPA and to ensure you pass and achieve the highest grade possible for you.

TASK

- Before your mock session, make a list of your strengths and areas that you need to develop.
- Make a plan of how you are going to achieve areas that you have identified that require development with a clear strategy.
- Research SMART targets and link this to the areas you have identified.

CASE STUDY

PC Peter Morris had successfully completed the 60 credits required to move through the gateway; he had achieved all necessary milestones with the police and university and was ready for his mock EPA. He received the meeting invite for the mock EPA from his designated coach two weeks before his final EPA and thought that he would remember all the detail in his portfolio, even though he had not engaged with it for over nine months. This was a very poor decision from PC Morris; he was not prepared for his mock and found the session difficult with many embarrassing pauses as he was unable to answer any of the questions posed by the coach. The coach reminded him that he was to undergo his final EPA in two weeks' time and if he did not prepare, he was very likely to fail one if not two elements of his EPA, which could have a significant impact on his apprenticeship and employment with the police. After the mock session had finished, he started to make a plan of how he would prepare for his EPA to ensure he would pass first time.

What is standardisation?

Standardising practice ensures all lecturers, trainers, assessors and quality assurers interpret and follow the requirements of the programme or qualification in the same way. It is also very important that all those involved are consistent and fair to all learners throughout their programme of study and work-based assessment. This enables all people involved to work as a team, supporting, guiding and giving an equitable service to all learners (Gravells, 2015). All learners are unique, and their learning experience and journey may be very different to others in their cohort, which must be considered when planning for assessments. This may mean differentiating some teaching, learning and assessment materials to suit the needs of each student officer. It is very important that a student officer undergoes an initial assessment either before or when they start their employment with their respective police force. This should not be limited to the beginning of the programme and should be an ongoing process as needs can change. If you feel that you require extra support during your programme, please inform your force and university and this can be implemented for you.

New recruits to the police service will have differing times of probation depending on which entry pathway they have taken to join the police (College of Policing, 2020b). The PCDA is a three-year programme of study; regardless of your entry programme, all student officers will be assigned a tutor, undergo workplace assessments, and be supported and guided by the assessment team within the training department to ensure that the Full Operational Competence (FOC) are complete. There will be robust processes in place to ensure that all student officers are being assessed consistently across the force and assessment decisions are regularly moderated by internal verifiers who moderate assessments and decisions made. The same robust process will be in place at the university you attend.

Standardisation of the EPA

Regular standardisation meetings will take place to ensure both consistency in decisions and a fair and robust quality process. After the EPA is completed, the IA must attend a standardisation meeting to discuss grades, passes and failures. They must explain how they have arrived at the grades that they have awarded for each component of the EPA with the quality team at the university; the grades are then agreed, ratified and then progress to a Board of Studies, where grades are confirmed and released to students.

Conclusion

Planning and preparing early for your EPA is imperative to ensure success throughout your programme of study and success in your final assessment. There is a wealth of support both at the university and with your employer, the police, to ensure that your learning journey is both successful and enjoyable. Ensure that you read and fully understand all assessment requirements and criteria to enable you to pass all required assessments with ease and move on to the next stage of your learning programme. Fully prepare for both your mock and final EPA to pass first time, obtain your degree in Professional Policing Practice and become a fully competent police officer.

6 EPA day: pass first time

> **LEARNING OBJECTIVES**
>
> After reading this chapter you will be able to:
>
> - understand the importance of planning and preparation before you take your end-point assessment;
> - explain the structure of the components of the end-point assessment and the assessment criteria for each component;
> - critically evaluate your own planning and preparation for the end-point assessment to ensure success in your final assessment.

Introduction

This chapter covers the importance of planning and preparation before the final end-point assessment (EPA) takes place. It looks in detail at the assessment elements, typical questions and suggestions of how to prepare and answer these questions with ease. Before you undergo the EPA, your Independent Assessor (IA) will have access to your police portfolio of evidence, including signed-off evidence logs from your Independent Patrol Status (IPS) and Full Operational Competence (FOC). Depending upon your police force, they may be stored on an online platform or will be PDFs uploaded into online folders for the IA to read through and prepare your EPA questions for the professional discussion element of the EPA.

The IA will spend a considerable amount of time reading through the evidence in your portfolio and will make notes and compile questions to ask you in the professional discussion. Therefore, it is very important that you are conversant with the content and ready to answer any questions relating to any of the evidence of incidents that you have attended in your portfolio. To ensure you are able to do this and recall information from evidence logs in your portfolio, you must revise and famiIarise yourself regularly with this information before the EPA takes place. The EPA is an opportunity to discuss with your IA the incidents you attended, why you made the decisions that you did and to reflect on how you could improve your response if you attended that incident again. There is no trickery; if you are knowledgeable and have a well-organised portfolio, your EPA will be an enjoyable experience. If you do not prepare and do not use the feedback from your mock and coaching session to plan and revise for your final EPA, it could be a very difficult assessment for you.

Remember – you must successfully answer each of the 13 questions asked by the IA to pass and achieve the professional discussion element of the EPA. You will be graded on your answers and given an overall grade for the element. This is discussed in detail in this chapter with detail of how to obtain a distinction grade.

The IA will also read and grade your evidence-based research project (EBRP) before you undertake the presentation and panel element and will also read your presentation slides before you present to the panel. They will also prepare questions for this element of your EPA. This is also covered in depth later on in this chapter.

The structure of your EPA

There are different ways that your final EPA may be set up depending on your collaborating force and higher education institutions. The assessment criteria are the same regardless, but they may be in a different format as detailed below.

- The EPA is conducted in one block assessment. You will have your professional discussion first, a short break and then will complete your presentation and panel discussion. This assessment block will be approximately three hours in duration.

- The EPA will be spilt into two components for assessment – the professional discussion for your first assessment and two weeks later your presentation of your EBRP findings and a panel interview.

Feedback from all parties who have been through the PCDA EPA process has been extremely positive for both structures of EPAs, but many students have preferred to have the assessment in one sitting. You will be informed how your EPA will be structured when you progress to Year 3. This information should also be detailed in your course handbook and EPA module handbook at university.

Be mindful that it can be a difficult logistical process to plan the EPAs due to the number of people that need to attend your assessment. There will be four people involved in your presentation panel element – you, the IA and representatives from the police and university – so it is very important that you inform the police/admin of your availability in the assessment period. If there is an issue when you have been allocated an assessment slot, you must inform the police/admin as soon as possible to rearrange.

All assessment sessions are recorded for moderation and quality purposes and you will be notified when the recording of the session starts and ends.

Preparing for your EPA

Independent Assessor top tips to prepare for your final EPA day

1. Ensure that when you receive your EPA invite from admin, you accept the invite as soon as practicable and make a note of the date and time in your diary or calendar. There have been occasions where students have failed to show up for their EPA as they had not checked their emails or just forgot. If you do not attend your EPA, a zero fail grade will be recorded on your grading document unless there was a mitigating circumstance that prevented you from attending (evidence may be requested to prove this event).

2. Make a plan regarding any areas of weakness/knowledge gaps that were identified during your mock EPA and ensure that you are fully ready to take your final EPA. Feedback from your mock EPA is a positive process designed to support and guide you to achieve the grade that you aspire to achieve. The mock and coaching session is your opportunity to practise some aspects of the assessment and identify any areas that could be improved. Students who do not attend their mock session or do not implement the advice given to help them improve achieve significantly lower grades or fail components of their EPA.

3. Ensure that you are fully prepared, your portfolio is in order and notes are at hand to assist you through your EPA. Plan at least a month ahead to revisit your portfolio, make notes for each of the assessment areas and revise any definitions that you are likely to be asked during the assessment. If you plan, the EPA can be an enjoyable process where you confidently answer each question with ease.

4. Have your ID ready and to hand when it is requested at the start of your assessment. Some students forget and then get very flustered while the panel watch them pull apart their living room or bag trying to find it. We are unable to start the assessment without viewing your ID.

5. First impressions count; this is your official final assessment for your police apprenticeship so professional dress and appearance is required. Some forces may require you to wear your police uniform or others may request business attire, so carefully read your joining instructions/requirements before the assessment.

6. Have a drink available to hand for when the assessment is taking place. A good tactic if you need some time to think after a question is posed is to have a drink of water. The IA will be happy for you to have a drink throughout your assessment.

7. The location of your assessment is very important and can have a significant impact on your assessment if not suitable. If you are in work at a police station, ensure that you are in a quiet location where you will not be disturbed. Put a note on the door that an examination is taking place requesting that you are not disturbed. If you are at home or at another location away from work, ensure that you will not be disturbed, no animals are in the room and your mobile phone is switched off or on mute.

8. Log on to your meeting early to check that your IT is working. By logging on early you will be able to seek help if you are experiencing any IT issues before the session officially starts. If the EPA is in person, ensure that you are there early to prepare and set out your portfolio and notes on the table in the room.

9. It is time to shine! Be ready to start your assessment as soon as the meeting starts; take a deep breath and smile. Be confident and ready to share all the amazing accomplishments that you have achieved during your PCDA programme with your IA and panel.

Assessment 1: professional discussion

Following through the gateway, after successful completion of your Operational Competence Portfolio (OCP), you will be required to engage in a professional discussion. The IA will review your OCP before the professional discussion element of the EPA and will have prepared questions regarding the evidence of incidents you attended in your portfolio. The professional discussion will last approximately 60–75 minutes. The IA will assess the application of all core workplace-based policing knowledge, skills and behaviours (KSBs) that are required to successfully achieve the professional discussion element of the EPA. It is very important that you prepare and are knowledgeable about the evidence in your portfolio as your IA might request you to talk about an incident you attended two years ago and want to discuss specific detail with you. The professional discussion comprises 13 questions, all of which you must successfully answer, and you will have approximately five minutes to answer each question.

The professional discussion element will be graded as distinction, pass or fail; the pass grade for this and other elements of the EPA is 50 per cent. The key assessment criteria that underpin the KSBs (which apply to your OCP) are shown below with examples and suggestions to help you prepare for your EPA. To assist you in the assessment, the assessment criteria are clearly stated in each question so that you are aware of what the IA is assessing against.

Top tip

Listen carefully to what you are being asked by the IA. Are they asking you to choose your example or are they referring to an evidence log in your portfolio?

A common mistake is that students are in a rush to answer the question without really listening to what the question they are being asked actually is. This causes issues and students then go off on a tangent, run out of time and do not successfully answer the question. Listen to the question posed by the IA; if you are not sure what is being asked or you require some clarification, you must ask. If you do go off topic the IA will try to bring you back on track with targeted questioning if possible.

Professional discussion questions and examples

Shown below are the 13 assessment criteria that will be covered in the professional discussion element of the EPA (IfATE, 2017). There are some example questions to show you how the IA chooses examples from your portfolio for your assessment; they will clearly state the evidence number so you can refer to this incident with your portfolio in hand. Each question has helpful tips and what the IA is expecting from you when you answer each question posed.

Question 1

Assessment criteria 1	Candidates will be able to demonstrate the following to evidence competence	Question and comments
Operating in accordance with the law, authorised professional practice and the code of ethics	In the operational policing workplace, demonstrate knowledge and understanding of the legal and professional practice requirements relating to the professional policing activities set out in II to IX below (this assessment document) having due regard to the Code of Ethics and the National Decision Model (NDM).	Evidence 12: You attended a report of a man threatening members of the public with a large knife in central Birmingham. • How did you use the NDM to inform your actions when dealing with this incident? • Can you give me an example of when the Code of Ethics has influenced a decision that you have taken?

What is your Independent Assessor looking for?

This question is asking you to outline a situation in which you have applied the National Decision Model (NDM) and Code of Ethics to inform your actions and decisions at that incident.

Points to consider

- You must link your answer to each stage of the NDM.
- You must demonstrate and articulate your thought process using the NDM and consideration of the Code of Ethics in relation to the incident that you are discussing with the IA.
- Many students start this question going into too much descriptive detail about the incident and so do not work around the NDM, meaning that they fail to complete the answer.
- You have approximately five minutes to answer this question so be mindful of time.
- Give short and concise answers. Consider whether your answer is relevant to the question posed.

Recap of the NDM (underpinned by the Code of Ethics)

- Gather information and intelligence.
- Assess threat and risk and develop a working strategy.
- Consider powers and policy.
- Identify options and contingencies.
- Take action and review what happened.

Question 2

Assessment criteria 2	Candidates will be able to demonstrate the following to evidence competence	Question and comments
Providing an initial response to policing incidents	Provide an initial response to incidents in line with legal and professional practice requirements including: • using the THRIVE approach; • communicating effectively with those at the scene; • controlling incidents, preserving the scene and potential evidence; • recognising and providing support to vulnerable individuals (including casualties); • providing support to victims and witnesses of the incident; • engaging in appropriate multi-agency referrals; • recording actions taken.	**Generic question example** Can you give me an example of an incident at which you provided an initial response where you recognised that you may need to provide support to victims/vulnerable individuals? • Outline your use of THRIVE in this example. • Who did/could you refer them to?

What is your Independent Assessor looking for?

This question is asking you to outline a situation where you provided an initial response using the THRIVE approach.

Points to consider

- You must link your answer to each element of the THRIVE approach.
- How did you communicate with those at the scene?
- How did you recognise and provide support to vulnerable people (including casualties, victims and witnesses) at the scene?
- Did you action any multi-agency referrals at this incident?
- If no, to whom could you refer them to for assistance after this incident?

Recap of the THRIVE approach

- **T**hreat.
- **H**arm.
- **R**isk.
- **I**nvestigation.
- **V**ulnerability.
- **E**ngagement.

Question 3

Assessment criteria 3	Candidates will be able to demonstrate the following to evidence competence	Question and comments
Managing conflict in a professional policing context	Apply conflict management and personal safety techniques with issued equipment, including: • making threat assessments using all available information; • using approved and appropriate communication techniques; • recognising danger cues; • applying appropriate and proportionate tactical options and conflict management techniques; • recording all actions taken and decisions made in line with legal and organisational procedures.	Evidence 21: You attended a report of a man who had assaulted his friend in a pub. He was very drunk and aggressive when you attended the location and had warning markers for weapons and violence. • How did you deal with this situation? • Would you deal with this incident any differently if you were to attend again today?

What is your Independent Assessor looking for?

This question is asking you to outline a situation in which you have applied conflict management techniques and personal safety techniques (with issued equipment).

Points to consider

- Ensure that you discuss what happened before the incident. What threat assessment did you make from the available information before you attended the incident?
- What was the situation when you arrived? What communication tactics did you use?
- What were the danger cues?
- How did you deal with the situation?
- How did you record actions and decisions made during the incident?
- What did you learn from this experience?
- On reflection, could you have dealt with this situation differently? What would you do differently if you had to deal with this situation today after your reflection?

Question 4

Assessment criteria 4	Candidates will be able to demonstrate the following to evidence competence	Question and comments
Providing support to vulnerable people, victims and witnesses	• Communicate effectively with vulnerable people, victims and witnesses. • Provide appropriate support to vulnerable people, victims and witnesses. • Demonstrate an understanding of the factors pertaining to vulnerable individuals, victims and witnesses that may influence their ability and willingness to receive support. • Assess the resilience and capability of the individual, and provide further support (including referrals) as appropriate.	Evidence 1: You attended a report of a burglary. The IP was elderly, vulnerable and a repeat victim of crime. • How did you identify them as vulnerable? • How would you define vulnerability? • What support is available for vulnerable victims of crime?

What is your Independent Assessor looking for?

This question is asking you to outline an occasion where you provided support to vulnerable people, victims and witnesses.

Points to consider

- Ensure you that you are prepared to discuss an example of an incident that you attended where you offered and provided support to a vulnerable person (this can be a victim or a witness).
- How would you define vulnerability?
- How did you identify them as vulnerable?
- Why is it important that you treat vulnerable people with empathy?
- What support is available to help vulnerable people? Who did you refer the vulnerable person to after dealing with this incident?
- On reflection, would you deal with this situation any differently today?

Question 5

Assessment criteria 5	Candidates will be able to demonstrate the following to evidence competence	Question and comments
Using police powers to deal with suspects	• Arrest and detain suspects in line with legal and organisational requirements and timescales.	Evidence 7: You arrested a 15-year-old boy who had caused damage to a fence in his local neighbourhood.

| | • Report suspects in line with legal and organisational requirements and timescales.
• Apply alternative options with regard to disposal of suspects, in line with organisational requirements. | • What disposal options were open to you when dealing with this incident?
• How did you arrive at the decisions that you made? |

What is your Independent Assessor looking for?

This question is asking you to consider your police powers to deal with suspects.

Points to consider

- Ensure that you are prepared to be asked a range of questions regarding the arrest, detention and reporting of suspects.
- Consider an incident that you attended where you applied alternative options with regard to disposal of suspects, in line with organisational requirements such as a cannabis warning, etc.
- What disposal options were open to you in dealing with this incident?
- How did you arrive at the decision that you took?
- Reflecting on this decision, would you make the same decision today?

Question 6

Assessment criteria 6	Candidates will be able to demonstrate the following to evidence competence	Question and comments
Conducting police searches	Conduct safe, lawful and effective police searches of premises, vehicles and outside spaces including: • communicating appropriately with those at the search scene; • identifying the correct search areas; • protecting search scenes; • preventing loss or contamination of potential evidence; • utilising approved search techniques; • analysing the significance of items found during the search; • seizing items covered by identified search powers; • maintaining the integrity of seized items; • leaving the search scene in the required condition; • documenting all decisions, actions, options and rationales.	Evidence 32: You were tasked to assist with an outdoor area search for a five-year-old boy who had been missing from his home address for 12 hours. • How did you plan and carry out this search?

What is your Independent Assessor looking for?

This question is asking you to outline a search of a premises, vehicle or outside space which was safe, lawful and effective.

Points to consider

- Ensure that you are fully prepared to discuss an example of an incident from your portfolio that relates to searching a premise, vehicle or outdoor space.
- How did you plan for and carry out this search?
- How did you ensure your actions were in accordance with the Code of Ethics?
- Why is it important to ensure there is no loss or contamination of potential evidence at the scene?
- On reflection, if you carried out that search again, what would you do differently or how would you improve your searching practice?

Question 7

Assessment criteria 7	Candidates will be able to demonstrate the following to evidence competence	Question and comments
Conducting police searches of individuals	Conduct police searches of individuals in line with legal and organisational requirements including: • using authorised and appropriate systematic search methods; • communicating appropriately with the individual before and during the search; • controlling individuals in order to prevent loss or contamination of evidence, escape of individual(s) and/or harm to any person; • maintaining personal safety using approved and appropriate techniques; • seizing any identified items covered by the relevant search power; • maintaining the integrity of seized items; • informing individuals being searched of the results of the search and any further actions to be taken; • documenting all decisions, actions, options and rationale.	Using any of the examples in your portfolio or any other example that you wish to introduce, outline an occasion where you have searched an individual.

What is your Independent Assessor looking for?

This question is asking you to outline a police search of an individual in line with legal and organisational requirements.

Points to consider

- This could be a generic question or an example from your portfolio – using any of the examples in your portfolio or any other example you wish to introduce, outline an occasion where you have searched an individual.
- Why is it important to communicate with the person that you are searching? What information do you need to discuss with them before, during and after the search process?
- How has your understanding of search techniques developed since training school?
- On reflection, if you were to carry out this search again today what would you do differently?

Question 8

Assessment criteria 8	Candidates will be able to demonstrate the following to evidence competence	Question and comments
Conducting priority and volume investigations	Conduct priority and volume investigations including: • planning and conducting an initial investigation; • gathering information, intelligence and evidence to support investigation; • undertaking investigative and evidential evaluation throughout the investigation; • briefing relevant others regarding the progress of the investigation; • identifying the need for any other additional support, including escalation; • identifying and working with victims, potential witnesses and suspects; • dealing with suspects in line with investigative decision-making; • providing victims, witnesses and their families with information, support and protection in accordance with their needs; • retaining and recording the details of an investigation.	In your role as a police officer you will have to plan and conduct initial investigations. • Can you give me an example of when you have done this? • Outline your investigation plan in this case. • How did you ensure that the needs of the victim were met?

What is your Independent Assessor looking for?

This question is asking you to outline an incident that you attended where you conducted the initial planning of an investigation.

Points to consider

- Outline your investigation plan in this case.
- How did you gather information, intelligence and evidence to support this investigation?

- Why did you carry out the investigation process in the way that you did?
- How did you ensure that the needs of the victim were met?
- On reflection, would you do anything different if you dealt with this investigation again? What could you improve?

Question 9

Assessment criteria 9	Candidates will be able to demonstrate the following to evidence competence	Question and comments
Interviewing victims, witnesses and suspects	Plan and prepare interviews with victims, witnesses and suspects. Conduct interviews with victims, witnesses and suspects including: • explaining the interview process to those present and confirming understanding; • maintaining the security and welfare of those present; • using approved interview and communication techniques to obtain accurate accounts; • using exhibits in line with approved interview techniques; • addressing any contingencies that may arise during the interview; • completing all necessary documents and records; • closing the interview, informing all present of the next steps.	Evidence 11: You interviewed a victim of domestic abuse. • How did you plan for this interview?
	And, for suspect interviews: • delivering pre-interview briefings to legal representatives; • using the required cautions, evidential or special warnings and checking the suspect's understanding; • evaluate interviews with victims, witnesses and suspects and carrying out post-interview procedures.	Evidence 12: You conducted suspect interview with a man who had been arrested on suspicion of harassment of his ex-partner. • How did you plan for this interview?

What is your Independent Assessor looking for?

This question is in two parts – victim and witnesses and suspect interviews – so be mindful when planning your answers, including consideration of timings.

Points to consider

Victim and witness interviews
- You will need to prepare an example of a time when you interviewed a victim or witness from your portfolio or a more recent example if asked by your IA.

- Consider how you planned for this. Did you need to take anything into account before or during the interview? Childcare etc?
- How did you conduct the interview? What interview/communication techniques did you use to get the best available evidence from the interview?

Suspect interviews
- How do you plan for a suspect interview?
- Use the PEACE Model – **P**lanning and preparation, **E**ngage and explain, **A**ccount clarification and challenge, **C**losure and **E**valuation.
- How would you respond if the suspect gives a no comment answer throughout the interview?
- How has your interview technique improved throughout your apprenticeship?

Question 10

Assessment criteria 10	Candidates will be able to demonstrate the following to evidence competence	Question and comments
Response policing	Provide an effective initial response to a critical incident.	Evidence 15: You attend an address after reports of a domestic violence incident. This is a common occurrence at this address and there are two young children at the address. The violence has got progressively worse with the male attacking his female partner on multiple occasions. • What is your definition of a critical incident? • How might this incident fit that definition?

What is your Independent Assessor looking for?

This question is asking you to discuss an example where you provided an effective initial response to a critical incident.

Points to consider

- Consider an example of when you provided an effective response to a critical incident (CI).
- Be prepared to give a definition of a CI to your IA if they ask you.
- If the example discussed was not a CI when you initially arrived, how did it escalate? What did you do? What happened to make you consider that this may become a CI?

- How did you prioritise your actions in dealing with this incident?
- Self-reflect on the incident. What went well? What did not go so well? How can you improve next time you encounter a similar incident?

Question 11

Assessment criteria 11	Candidates will be able to demonstrate the following to evidence competence	Question and comments
Policing communities	• Communicate and engage proactively with communities, including through use of social media. • Foster productive partnerships in community policing.	In your role as a police officer it is important that you foster productive partnerships with local communities. • Can you give an example of this? • How might the police use social media to effectively engage with communities?

What is your Independent Assessor looking for?

This question is in two parts and can be linked if the example you use in your portfolio is linked. If they are not linked, think of two examples from your portfolio or more recent examples that you can discuss with your IA.

Points to consider

Communicate and engage proactively with communities, including through use of social media

- Consider incidents or tasking that you have been involved in that required you to use social media such as Twitter or Facebook to engage with the community.
- Good examples could be a missing person or a crime reduction initiative that the community could assist with. What did you do? What was the overall result when engaging proactively with the community in your force area?

Foster productive partnerships in community policing

- Consider why it is important to build a good relationship with the community that you serve.
- Think of examples in your portfolio and more recent examples of where you have worked with the community.
- What could be the consequences of not building good relationships with the community? What could be the likely outcome?

Question 12

Assessment criteria 12	Candidates will be able to demonstrate the following to evidence competence	Question and comments
Information and intelligence	• Conduct effective analysis and evaluation of information and intelligence. • Develop information and intelligence to inform the tasking and co-ordination process.	In your role as a police officer it is important that when you conduct inquiries and investigations you obtain information and intelligence to assist you with the task. • Can you give me an example of this? • Can you give an example where you have gathered information/intelligence that has supported the tasking process?

What is your Independent Assessor looking for?

This question is asking you to discuss examples of when you conducted effective analysis and evaluation of information and intelligence. The question also covers you developing information and intelligence to inform the tasking and co-ordination process.

Points to consider

- The assessment criteria for Question 12 may seem more complicated to answer than other questions posed in the professional discussion assessment. Put simply, you conduct effective analysis and evaluation of information and intelligence for the majority of jobs that you will attend.
- It is simply asking you to consider an incident that you have attended/dealt with where you had to assess information and intelligence that is relevant and which can assist you with your inquiry or investigation. This could be from gathering evidence from witness statements or scrutinising force systems.
- Can you give an example where you have gathered information/intelligence that has supported the tasking process?

Question 13

Assessment criteria 13	Candidates will be able to demonstrate the following to evidence competence	Question and comments
Conducting investigations	• Demonstrate appropriate strategies for dealing with more complex police interviews. • Apply appropriate investigative procedures in respect of internet-facilitated crime.	Can you give an example from your portfolio or more recently of a complex interview that you have been involved in? • How did you plan for and carry out this interview? • What challenge did this present and how did you overcome this? • How have you secured evidence digitally using this example above or another case?

What is your Independent Assessor looking for?

This question is seeking to find an example of a complex interview that you have conducted. The IA may have chosen one from your portfolio that they have identified as complex. What could be deemed as complex? Maybe there was a language barrier with the person that you were interviewing and you needed an interpreter to assist with the interview? Or were there many involved in the incident?

Points to consider

Demonstrate appropriate strategies for dealing with more complex police interviews
- Why was it complex?
- What strategies did you consider or implement to deal with this complex interview?
- How did you plan for this interview?
- What were the challenges when dealing with this interview and how did you overcome these challenges?

Apply appropriate investigative procedures in respect of internet-facilitated crime
- If you have not covered appropriate investigative procedures in respect of internet-facilitated crime in any of the other questions you will be asked this question here.
- How did you investigate internet-facilitated crime?
- How did you secure digital evidence in this example or another case?
- What can be the challenges?
- Self-reflection – if you were to deal with this complex police interview again or investigative procedures for internet-facilitated crime, what would you do differently? What went well? What can you improve?

Grade descriptors for the professional discussion assessment examples

Table 6.1 An example of a grading decision for the professional discussion

Grade	Grading description	Met	Comments
Distinction (70% and over)	As pass below and: Valid and robust evidence of the student demonstrating an approach that is measurably beyond the minimum required standard for a complex/critical operation		

	situation. The student will be able to clearly explain how they have achieved the best possible outcome in the situation, going beyond what could be reasonably expected in the extenuating circumstances. Demonstrates adaptability to a challenging situation, decision-making and critical thinking 'outside the box'.		
Pass (50–69%)	All 13 (100%) of the required assessment criteria underpinning operational competence have been successfully met. The student has successfully met the minimum standard for all nationally set assessment criteria for the measurement of operational competence. A professional discussion following a review of the OCP has confirmed that the student is safe, lawful and operationally competent against all 13 of the specified assessment areas.	✓	*PC Morris was very well prepared for his professional discussion element of the EPA. Articulate with good communication skills. All underpinning operational competencies have been successfully met in the 13 required assessment criteria. Well done!* *Grade awarded: 58%*
Fail (0–49%)	One or more of the 13 required assessment criteria underpinning operational competence has not been met (less than 100%). The student has not successfully met the minimum standard for all nationally set assessment criteria for the measurement of operational competence and/or insufficient evidence is available to confirm via a professional discussion that all the assessment criteria have been successfully met. The student is not safe, has acted unlawfully and/or is not operationally competent against all 13 of the specified assessment areas.		

Assessment 2: evidence-based research project (EBRP)

This assessment is covered in detail in Chapter 4. This element of the EPA will have already been assessed and completed before your EPA day. The IA will have also marked and graded your research project before the presentation and panel discussion element of the EPA.

Assessment 3: presentation and panel discussion

Following completion of the EBRP, all students will be required to deliver a presentation of their research projects and take part in a panel discussion. You will present your findings during your presentation and then you will be asked questions by the panel regarding your EBRP and the presentation that they have just observed. The panel discussion also permits a final opportunity to assess the apprentice against areas (of the standard) where further clarity is required. It is for the IA to judge whether or not this is required (IfATE, 2017).

Top tips

1. Read the assessment criteria and guidance detailed in the module handbook and assignment brief. Many students do not read the assessment requirements or understand what is expected to be produced to meet the learning objectives for the assessment. When this occurs, it can have a detrimental effect on the grade awarded. If you require more clarity or advice on this part of your assessment, contact your module leader or look at the module on the VLE for further guidance.

2. The assessment guidelines and requirements on the assignment brief are a guide to assist you to produce a presentation that will include the required components in the allocated time. If the assessment guidance states no more than ten slides, follow the guidance. Some students ignore the guidance issued and produce more slides and as a consequence cannot complete the assessment in the allocated time and fail the EPA element. As previously stated, everyone involved in the assessment of your EPA wants you to achieve and pass the assessment with a high grade; follow the guidance available.

3. Ensure the presentation slides are aesthetically pleasing and easy to read. Even though you are not specifically required to produce a PowerPoint presentation it is a good medium to use. The points on each slide are easy prompts for your discussion in your presentation to the panel. If your EPA is online, practise sharing your slides on Teams or Zoom before the session; it can be both frustrating to the student and panel if there are issues with sharing because it is a new process not practised before the day.

4. Produce a professional presentation that shows that you have spent time thoughtfully composing and writing the presentation; first impressions count again with this element of the EPA. Use colour and pictures when required and produce a presentation to be proud of. You should have a clear title page and introduction to the presentation.

5. Ensure the font is clear and not too small for the panel to read and understand. The points on your slides are prompt points for you to discuss your findings to the panel rather than the full content. Know your content and present with confidence and conviction. This is your research and you should be able to present freely without looking at your notes and having your head down for the majority of your presentation.

6. Reference all your sources of information on your slides so it is clear what the sources are. Have a separate reference slide at the end of the presentation detailing all sources.
7. Practise delivering and presenting your EBRP presentation with a family friend or family member. It is very important that you have a practice session before your EPA to gauge timings of your presentation and that you adhere to the time allocated for your assessment.
8. Print out a copy of your presentation with notes and read it before your assessment. Have this to hand during the presentation so you are prepared to talk about the next slide or as a prompt.

Presentation

The presentation element of the assessment will typically be 30 minutes in length and should be delivered using PowerPoint or another method of visually presenting your project. Throughout this process, you are expected to critically analyse and reflect on:

- the foundation provided by operational competence;
- the application of higher-level skills, knowledge and behaviours to your work;
- the relevance of your project findings for operational delivery, indicating key learning points and recommendations;
- how you might synthesise your project findings into operational delivery, indicating key learning points and improvements to your own and others' working practices.

Each presentation will be unique to each student and EBRP carried out; however, the following broad areas should be considered for your presentation.

- What is the title and outline of your EBRP?
- What was your research question/hypothesis you were aiming to answer/test?
- What data did you use? Primary or secondary data? Interviews? Focus groups? Redacted police data? Something else? If you conducted primary research how many participants did you include?
- Describe how your EBRP maps across with the required KSBs.
- Outline the chronological timeline of your EBRP – when did you start? What did you do? When did you complete your EBRP?
- What challenges, ethical and professional, did you have completing your research? Describe any other issues that you had to consider (such as difficulty in obtaining reliable data).
- What lessons have been learnt from previous research? Link this to your EBRP introduction/literature review – what have other academic researchers and other police forces found previously?
- What were your findings/results? Are they what you expected? If not, why not?

- How does this research relate to your own area of work in policing?
- What are your recommendations for future research nationally and your force?

Panel discussion

The panel discussion will last approximately 30–40 minutes. The panel will include the IA, an academic member of university staff (likely to be your supervisor) and a member of your employing police force.

The panel discussion will ask you questions regarding your EBRP presentation and will review and permit the following.

- How core policing KSBs have underpinned your work.
- How higher-level skills and knowledge has been applied in the work-based setting.
- How you approached the work and dealt with any issues that arose.
- A detailed exploration of aspects of your project work, for example how can your recommendations add value to your force?
- Confirmation of the demonstration of appropriate interpersonal and behavioural skills within policing.
- This will also be the final opportunity to assess you against any KSBs where further clarity is required.

What could you be asked in the panel discussion?

The panel will likely ask you bespoke questions regarding your research and presentation but will have similar themes for each student. You should consider the points outlined below, which are linked to the different sections of your EBRP. These can assist you with the layout of your presentation.

Introduction

1. Was the purpose of your project clearly explained?
2. What was the research question/hypothesis you were working to prove?
3. Were the project's aims clear?
4. How did the research fit with the priorities of your police force?

Literature review

1. What level of research was attempted?
2. Did you demonstrate critical analysis in your research?
3. How detailed and thorough was the analysis?
4. Was the research valid and recent?

5. What was the level of knowledge exhibited?
6. Was the referencing appropriate and correctly cited?

Methodology

1. What method was used and why?
2. How had the research been planned and carried out?
3. Were the strengths and weaknesses of this method outlined?

Results/findings

1. What were the findings?
2. Have these findings been critically analysed?
3. Overall, how valid are they?

Discussion

1. What conclusions can be drawn from the research findings?
2. Are the conclusions reached balanced/fair and supported by the findings?
3. Do the conclusions relate to current policies and practice of your employing police force – will change be required?
4. Were the aims of the presentation met?

Implications/recommendations

1. Have you any academic recommendations (areas for further research)?
2. What are your recommendations that could be implemented in your police force or other agencies?

General/throughout

1. How does the EBRP link with the KSBs?

The Independent Assessor has final responsibility for assessment decisions

The IA will lead and chair the panel discussion. Usually the panel will meet before the assessment to decide what bespoke questions you will be asked after reading your EBRP and having a preview of your presentation slides. You will be asked questions by all members of the panel during this assessment. The IA will sign off the assessment of the presentation and panel discussion and award the final grade for this assessment after discussion with the panel members. In Table 6.2 you will see the grading criteria that the IA will use to grade your presentation and panel discussion. Be mindful of this criteria when planning for your assessment.

Table 6.2 Assessment guidance for presentation and panel component of the EPA

Grade	Grading description
Distinction (70% and above)	As 'Pass' and: The student has evidenced a comprehensive understanding of how core policing KSBs have underpinned their project, and higher-level skills and knowledge have been successfully applied and adapted to a complex or critical situation within their chosen area of specialist professional practice. The student can clearly evidence, explain or demonstrate how the application of appropriate interpersonal and behavioural skills has permitted them to achieve the best possible outcome in extenuating circumstances. The student's approach to their work has been safe and lawful, and they have addressed any issues that arose within the limits of their role and responsibility, while thoroughly evaluating alternative courses of action and the advantages and disadvantages of each.
Pass (50–69%)	The student has explained or demonstrated how core policing KSBs have underpinned their project, and evidence of how higher-level skills and knowledge have been applied in their chosen area of specialist professional practice is evident. The student has explained or demonstrated how appropriate interpersonal and behavioural skills have been consistently applied within their role as a PC. The student's approach to their work has been safe and lawful, and they have addressed any issues that arose within the limits of their role and responsibility. They can account for changes they have made to their own working practices.
Fail (0–49%)	The student has not been able to explain or demonstrate how core KSBs have underpinned their project, and there is no clear evidence of how higher-level skills and knowledge have been applied in the work-based setting. The student has not been able to explain or demonstrate how appropriate interpersonal and behavioural skills have been applied within a policing context. The student's approach to their work has been unsafe or unlawful, and they have failed to address any issues that arose.

CASE STUDIES

Jack

PC Jack Maher failed to attend his allocated appointment slot for his mock EPA session with a coach to prepare for his final EPA, which was scheduled to take place two weeks after the mock. He did not contact admin or email the coach to inform them that he was unable to make the appointment; when challenged why he did not attend by his personal tutor, he said '*I don't need to, I know what I am doing.*'

On his EPA day, he was late for the online assessment session and stated that he had stuff to do that was more important, but he was here now. He did not offer an apology and looked like he had just got out of bed; he was wearing a grey tracksuit which looked like it had food down the front and his hair had not been brushed. The IA requested to see his ID before the assessment for the professional discussion element could commence. Jack looked confused and said that he had not got any ID with him to hand and requested if he could do this later. After his request was refused, he spent five minutes in another room trying to find his passport.

Eventually he found it and the professional discussion finally started ten minutes late due to Jack's disorganisation.

Jack was not prepared for his professional discussion; he had not made any notes to assist him in the assessment. He had not prepared his portfolio of evidence to follow the assessment criteria for the assessment. This left him totally unprepared for the assessment and he could not locate the operational evidence in his portfolio when asked by the IA for specific detail. The first question regarding the NDM was met with a blank expression from Jack and a very uncomfortable silence. The IA tried to assist Jack with prompt points and tried to help him remember the incident. He attempted to answer but did not achieve the criteria set and so failed the first question. The IA worked his way through the professional discussion questions and Jack was only able to successfully answer one question. It was an extremely difficult 60 minutes for both the IA and PC Maher due to the lack of planning and preparation. Jack failed the professional discussion element of his EPA as he did not successfully achieve the assessment criteria in the 13 areas being assessed. The session was recorded and could be reviewed by the course leader and his police supervisor after they were informed by the IA that Jack had failed his assessment and that he was concerned by his conduct.

Jack passed his EPA on his second attempt after two coaching sessions and getting fully prepared for his next assessment attempt. He reflected on the feedback given by the IA and realised that 'trying to wing it' on his first attempt was not a good planning strategy.

Rich

PC Rich Chumley attended his online presentation and panel discussion assessment with a guest in the room, his dog Molly. The assessment panel comprised the IA, a training inspector from the police and his EBRP supervisor from university, who were not aware of the dog in the room at the start of the assessment. All checks and instructions were discussed before the start of the assessment and then Molly started to bark. The IA requested that the dog be removed from the room before the assessment started; Rich refused and said '*the dog stays where she is, she will be ok.*' The panel were surprised at the response from Rich, but all agreed that she was quiet now and the assessment could start when Rich was ready to upload his presentation on Teams and start his presentation.

During the presentation, the dog kept barking and jumping up at Rich and eventually knocked his laptop to the floor. The IA asked Rich to pause his presentation and to let the dog out of the room so that he would be able to focus on his presentation; he again refused. Rich was unable to finish his presentation in the allocated time due to the disruption by his dog and failed his presentation and panel discussion element. At the end of the assessment, he was asked by the panel if Molly was his support dog due to his refusal to remove her from the room during the assessment. He replied, '*No, I just don't want to hurt her feelings.*'

> Rich eventually passed his EPA on his second attempt, without his dog in the room.
>
> **Neema**
>
> PC Neema Patel was online early for her presentation and panel assessment as she was nervous about sharing her presentation slides online with the panel. Neema had forgotten to send her completed presentation slides to her tutor by the deadline, so the panel had not had sight of them before the assessment. Neema uploaded the slides with ease and the IA explained that she would have 30 minutes to present the findings of her research project to the panel. She would be given a five-minute warning if she was getting near to the allocated time for the assessment so that she could finish her presentation.
>
> The recommended number of slides for the presentation was around 10; Neema had produced 30 slides and when she was given her five-minute warning that the assessment time was soon to end, she had only presented eight slides. The presentation regarding Neema's research project was incomplete so she failed the assessment.
>
> Neema passed her assessment on the second attempt after a time management coaching session and condensing her 30 slides into a much more manageable 10 slides. She practised the presentation with her family before the reassessment to ensure it was within the 30-minute time allocation.

TASK

To prepare for your final EPA, it is important to revise and revisit your portfolio of evidence and link the incidents to your professional discussion assessment.

- Before you start this process, ensure that your portfolio is clearly labelled in order to assist you with the mapping process.
- Print out the professional discussion template and work through your portfolio, making notes on the template about examples of incidents that fit each assessment criteria question.
- When you have completed the assessment template, identify any knowledge gaps in each area and make a plan to find the information and include it in your notes.
- Plan your actual assessment notes at least a month in advance of your final EPA and regularly read them before the assessment day.

Awarding the EPA

Once all assessments have been completed (and graded), the process of standardisation will take place to ensure all quality requirements have been undertaken and adhered to for your programme. The PCDA is an integrated degree apprenticeship and aligns to the academic awards of the university, so an exam board takes place before grades are officially awarded. You will be given an overall grading of a distinction, pass or fail for the EPA. Table 6.3 describes how the EPA will be graded overall.

Table 6.3 Overall grading information for the EPA

Grade	Grading description
Distinction	The student has fully met the requisite competency-based criteria and synthesised key skills, knowledge and behaviours from their theoretical studies into their workplace activity. Additionally, they have demonstrated exceptional critical thought and/or approach to complex/critical situation(s) to achieve the best possible outcome in the situation, going beyond what could be reasonably expected of them. They have reflected on the application of the KSBs, assessed the likely outcomes of alternative approaches and demonstrated making changes to working practices through this reflection. The distinction-level descriptor of the OCP-based professional discussion must be met **and** both other assessment elements must be 70% or higher.
Pass	The student has fully met the requisite competency-based criteria and synthesised key skills, knowledge and behaviours from their theoretical studies into their workplace activity. Additionally, they have reflected on the application of these KSBs and demonstrated making changes to working practices through this reflection. OCP-based professional discussion: 100% of the assessment criteria has been met **and** both other assessment elements must be marked 50% or higher.
Fail	The student has failed one or more of the EPA's three required assessment elements. OCP-based professional discussion: less than 100% of the assessment criteria have been met **and/or** one or more of the other assessment elements is marked lower than 50%.

Conclusion

Effective planning and preparation for your final EPA will ensure that you are knowledgeable and confident to pass all elements of the EPA. This chapter has covered in depth all areas of the EPA day, with guidance on how to prepare effectively for each element. The chapter has also detailed the depth in which the IA assesses each element, starting with your OCP, your EBRP and also in person during your professional discussion and presentation and panel assessment. When you are prepared for your assessment, it is clearly evident to the IA and panel. The chapter has also detailed real case studies of student officers who were not prepared and as a consequence failed their EPA.

7 Programme and EPA overview and checklist

> **LEARNING OBJECTIVES**
>
> After reading this chapter you will be able to:
>
> - understand that planning for your end-point assessment starts at the beginning of your PCDA and throughout your three-year programme;
> - explain the importance of preparing well in advance for all elements of the end-point assessment;
> - critically analyse the requirement for self-reflection throughout your apprenticeship in order to succeed and pass your PCDA end-point assessment on the first attempt.

Key milestones

The need to plan and prepare is key to the successful completion of your PCDA programme. This chapter covers the important milestones that must be successfully completed and achieved during each year of the PCDA programme. The checklists for each year/element of your end-point assessment (EPA) are in an easy-to-navigate format in this chapter. As you work through each year of your PCDA, you can plan ahead for when you will achieve each milestone. This list is not exhaustive and you will have other tasks to complete along the way. There are some useful tips included in this chapter that have assisted students who have undertaken their EPA and have successfully passed first time. It is also a good idea to tick off each completed task as it will show you how far you have progressed from day one of your programme.

Year 1

By the end of Year 1 you must complete and achieve the following.

Number	Task	✓
1.	Off-the-job training (OTJT) tracker complete for Year 1. Full attendance at tripartite reviews.	
2.	All academic assignments and tasks complete and achieved. Any resits for failed elements are also complete and achieved.	
3.	Independent Patrol Status (IPS) complete and signed off by the police.	
4.	Full Operational Competence (FOC) police portfolio on track and signed off for Year 1.	
5.	Maths/English on track to complete if required to be taken?	

TASK

Congratulations, you have successfully completed Year 1! It is important that you now critically reflect on Year 1 as you progress to Year 2. Consider the following and make notes after reflecting on the following questions.

- What has gone well in Year 1?
- What has not gone so well in Year 1?
- How will you incorporate any learning from Year 1 into Year 2 to make an easy transition to Year 2 and level 5 of your PCDA programme?
- Make a plan using SMART targets for the forthcoming year. Consider if you require any support or guidance in any academic or operational areas of your PCDA programme.

Year 2

By the end of Year 2 you must complete and achieve the following.

Number	Task	✓
1.	Off-the-job training (OTJT) tracker complete for Year 2. Full attendance at tripartite reviews.	
2.	All academic assignments and tasks complete.	
3.	Full Operational Competencies complete and signed off.	
4.	Maths/English on track or complete if required to be taken?	

TASK

Congratulations, you have successfully completed Year 2! It is important that you now critically reflect on Year 2 as you progress to Year 3. Consider the following and make notes after reflecting on the following questions.

- What has gone well in Year 2?
- What has not gone so well in Year 2?
- Decide how you will incorporate any learning from Year 1 and 2 to make an easy transition to Year 3 and level 6 of your PCDA programme.
- Make a plan using SMART targets for the forthcoming year. Consider if you require any support or guidance in any academic or operational areas of your PCDA programme.
- Consider your favourite work-based learning placement this year and what area of policing that you would like to specialise in.
- Consider any areas of policing that you would like to research for your EBRP.

Year 3

To progress through the gateway in Year 3 you must complete and achieve the following.

Number	Task	✓
1.	Maths/English L2 functional skills achieved.	
2.	All academic assignments and tasks complete.	
3.	FOC portfolio complete and ready for mock and EPA.	
4.	Preparation for mock EPA.	
5.	Off-the-job training (OTJT) tracker up to date. Attend all tripartite reviews.	

To be ready to undertake your mock EPA you must complete and achieve the following.

Number	Task	✓
1.	Evidence-based research project (EBRP) complete.	
2.	Off-the-job training (OTJT) tracker is complete and up to date.	
3.	FOC portfolio fully complete, in order and labelled. You must regularly revise the contents of your portfolio as you could be asked questions in your professional discussion regarding any of the incidents that you attended.	
4.	Be prepared and plan as if this was your final EPA. Ensure you have notes and examples for each question. Practise timings for professional discussion questions and presentation findings of your EBRP.	
5.	Be smartly dressed and have a drink handy.	

6.	Ensure your location is quiet and you are free of distractions for your mock assessment.	
7.	Take any animals out of the room if you are at home and put them into another room.	

TASK

Make notes immediately after the mock EPA has taken place as this will help you plan for your final EPA.

- What went well?
- What did not go well?
- Where there any questions/areas in your mock that you need to revisit or revise before the final EPA day?
- Make a plan and action that plan promptly.

Your final EPA day

The following should be completed before your final EPA.

Number	Task	✓
1.	Check joining instructions – time and date.	
2.	Log on early to check that the IT is working. By logging on early you will be able to seek help if you are experiencing any IT issues.	
3.	Professional dress and appearance – first impressions count!	
4.	Have a drink available to hand – preferably water.	
5.	Have ID ready – passport/warrant card/driver's licence – and nearby to your computer.	
6.	Quiet location – ensure that you will not be disturbed. If at work put a note on the door that you are undertaking an assessment and are not to be disturbed. If you are at home or at another location from work, ensure that you won't be disturbed, no animals are in the room and your mobile phone is switched off or on mute.	
7.	Ensure that your notes/portfolio are tidy and available nearby to access when needed. Stick some notes on the wall (if available and the assessment is online) for prompt points such as THRIVE, NIM, definition of a critical incident etc. If your assessment is face to face with your Independent Assessor (IA) and panel, ensure that your notes are laid out neatly and accessible around you.	
8.	Be ready to start as soon as the meeting starts; take a deep breath and smile. Be confident and ready to share all the amazing accomplishments that you have achieved during your PCDA programme with your IA and the panel. You can do this!	

Check the following at the start of your assessment.

Number	Task	✓
1.	Be ready to introduce yourself and smile! Eye contact with the IA and panel are important regardless of whether your assessment is online or face to face.	
2.	Show ID when requested to do so.	
3.	Listen to instructions and the information on the structure of your EPA. The IA will run through the structure and running order of your EPA and give timings for each section.	
4.	This is now your opportunity to ask any questions you may have if you are not sure of any element of the EPA. The IA will assume that you are happy and ready to go if you say that you have no questions. Remember – the IA is there to support you through the process and really wants you to succeed. They are not trying to trick you; they will only be asking questions regarding incidents that you have attended and the completed research project that you have written.	
5.	Have regular sips of a drink as you have lots of talking to do during your assessment.	
6.	The clock will start to run when you state that you are ready to go and start your assessment.	
7.	Be aware of your posture – sit upright and talk to the IA and panel with confidence and passion about your PCDA learner journey. Tell them how you have progressed through your apprenticeship to date. Be ready for critical self-reflection questions throughout your programme and how you have dealt with incidents that you have attended.	
8.	If you are unsure of a question or what your IA or panel member have asked you, ask them to clarify the question.	
9.	If you need a moment to compose yourself or to consider the question, have a quick drink.	

Prepare for the professional discussion element of your EPA (60–75 minutes in duration).

Number	Task	✓
1.	Have your EPA template with notes near to your computer.	
2.	For the professional discussion, you have approximately five minutes for each assessment criteria. This covers the underpinning knowledge, skills and behaviours (KSBs) and your operational competence. There are 13 areas which you will be asked questions on regarding your portfolio and operational competence. Be prepared! Make notes of jobs you have attended that would address the assessment criteria.	
3.	Listen to the question the IA is asking you; if unsure, ask for clarification before answering the question posed.	
4.	Short, concise answers are required; do not waffle. You will be wasting allocated time. If you are prepared, you will have clear answers to the question posed.	
5.	Your IA will ensure that you answer your question in the given time and will give you a prompt if the allocated time is coming to an end.	
6.	If you are going off track from the question asked, the IA may ask you a question to bring you back to the original question posed. Listen carefully to what the IA is asking you.	
7.	Make sure you have a sip of water throughout the professional discussion.	

Check the following in relation to the EBRP (before your EPA).

Number	Task	✓
1.	Read through and familiarise yourself with your research project before your presentation and panel assessment.	
2.	Print out and highlight any areas which you think they may ask you questions on after you have completed your presentation during the panel element of your assessment.	
3.	Break down areas and make notes for preparation for your panel assessment. • Why did you choose this topic? • What issues/difficulties did you face? • What methods did you use? • When conducting your literature review, what did you find interesting? Surprising? Were there any gaps? • What are your recommendations? • Consider the impact your research could have on operational policing.	

Checklist for your presentation and panel assessment element (60 minutes in duration).

Number	Task	✓
1.	When composing the presentation regarding your EBRP, ensure that you follow the assessment guidelines such as number of slides and slide layout.	
2.	Ensure you have a clear title page and introduction to your presentation.	
3.	Ensure the font is clear and not too small for the panel to read and understand. The points on your slides are prompt points for you to discuss your findings with the panel, not the full content.	
4.	Reference all your sources of information on your slides and provide your references on a separate slide at the end of your PowerPoint presentation.	
5.	Produce a professional presentation that shows that you have spent time composing and writing the presentation. Use colour and pictures when required and produce a presentation to be proud of.	
6.	Practise the presentation with a friend or family member – it is very important that you adhere to the time allocated for the presentation.	
7.	Before the EPA, ensure that you have printed out a copy of your presentation and made notes on this; read this before your actual assessment. If you are prepared, it will show during your assessment that you have prepared and are very knowledgeable regarding your research topic.	
8.	On the day you will be asked questions from the panel about your EBRP and your presentation that they have just observed. A reminder that the panel will comprise the IA, a university representative and a police representative.	
9.	Questions likely from the panel: IA – overview of your research topic; police – operational impact; university – questions on how you carried out your research.	

Preparation is key for your EPA, and you must be fully prepared and knowledgeable in all areas in which you are being assessed. If you do not prepare, there is a significant risk that you could fail one or more elements of the EPA. If this occurs, you will be required to resit the elements which you have not successfully achieved. By failing elements of your EPA, this will mean that the completion of your police apprenticeship will be extended and your final sign-off and graduation will be delayed. In the unlikely event that you need to resit any elements of your EPA, some tips are shown below.

Resit guidance

Number	Task	✓
1.	After the assessment, conduct a self-reflection exercise on how you think the assessment went. What went well? What did not go so well? What could you improve next time?	
2.	Read the feedback from the IA on the assessment form and compose an action plan for your next assessment. Do not ignore the points to improve and recommendations made by the IA; this will ensure that you do not make the same mistakes again.	
3.	If you require any support and guidance to improve areas before your next assessment, ask and make that appointment as soon as possible. There is a wealth of support available to you from both your university and the police, so ensure that you use that support.	
4.	Practise, practise, practise! And ensure that you are fully prepared to pass at the next opportunity.	
5.	Remember that you only have three attempts to successfully complete the EPA.	

Conclusion

It is imperative that you are fully prepared for your final EPA for the PCDA. If you plan well in advance, you will be confident and at ease in all elements of your EPA. This chapter has provided many tips and recommendations for you to consider at each stage of your learner journey during your three-year programme. When you complete each milestone as you progress through your PCDA programme, complete the tick list in this chapter and consider how much you have learned and developed since you started the apprenticeship on day one. Good luck.

References

Chartered Institute of Personnel and Development (CIPD) (2022) *Coaching and Mentoring*. [online] Available at: www.cipd.co.uk/knowledge/fundamentals/people/development/coaching-mentoring-factsheet#gref (accessed 16 December 2022).

College of Policing (2014) *Code of Ethics*. [online] Available at: https://assets.college.police.uk/s3fs-public/2021-02/code_of_ethics.pdf (accessed 16 December 2022).

College of Policing (2017) *Competency and Values Framework Guidance*. [online] Available at: https://assets.college.police.uk/s3fs-public/2020-11/competency_and_values_framework_guidance.pdf (accessed 16 December 2022).

College of Policing (2020a) *Policing Education Qualification Framework (PEQF)*. [online] Available at: www.college.police.uk/career-learning/policing-education-qualifications-framework-peqf (accessed 16 December 2022).

College of Policing (2020b) *Initial Entry Routes*. [online] Available at: https://assets.college.police.uk/s3fs-public/2021-02/peqf-learning-to-date.pdf (accessed 16 December 2022).

College of Policing (2022a) What Works Centre for Crime Reduction. [online] Available at: www.college.police.uk/research/what-works-centre-crime-reduction (accessed 16 December 2022).

College of Policing (2022b) Recognition of Prior Experience and Learning (RPL). [online] Available at: https://profdev.college.police.uk/recognition-prior-experience-learning/ (accessed 16 December 2022).

College of Policing (2022c) APP (Authorised Professional Practice). [online] Available at: www.college.police.uk/app (accessed 16 December 2022).

College of Policing (2022d) Evidence-based Policing. [online] Available at: www.college.police.uk/research/evidence-based-policing-EBP (accessed 16 December 2022).

College of Policing (2022e) Tutor/Tutor Constable. [online] Available at: https://profdev.college.police.uk/professional-profile/tutor-tutor-constable/ (accessed 16 December 2022).

Copley, S (2011) *Reflective Practice for Policing Students*. Exeter: Learning Matters.

Dewey, J (1933) *How We Think*. Boston, MA: D C Heath and Co.

Education and Skills Act 2008. [online] Available at: www.legislation.gov.uk/ukpga/2008/25/contents (accessed 16 December 2022).

Education and Skills Funding Agency (ESFA) (2022a) Review Apprenticeship Progress. [online] Available at: www.gov.uk/government/publications/provider-guide-to-delivering-high-quality-apprenticeships/ongoing-apprenticeship-delivery (accessed 16 December 2022).

Education and Skills Funding Agency (ESFA) (2022b) Apprenticeship Gateway and Resits for End-point Assessment (EPA). [online] Available at: www.gov.uk/guidance/apprenticeship-gateway-and-resits-for-end-point-assessment-epa (accessed 16 December 2022).

Equality Act 2010. [online] Available at: www.legislation.gov.uk/ukpga/2010/15/contents (accessed 16 December 2022).

Gravells, A (2015) Standardisation. [online] Available at: www.anngravells.com/information/standardisation (accessed 16 December 2022).

Hills, D (2011) *Critical Thinking in an Hour*. Richmond: Trotman Publishing.

HM Government (2022a) Police Apprenticeships and Traditional Entry Programmes. [online] Available at: www.joiningthepolice.co.uk/application-process/ways-in-to-policing/apprenticeship-and-traditional-entry-programmes (accessed 16 December 2022).

HM Government (2022b) What Are the Benefits of an Apprenticeship? [online] Available at: www.apprenticeships.gov.uk/apprentices/benefits-apprenticeship (accessed 16 December 2022).

HM Government (2022c) Training Your Apprentice. [online] Available at: www.apprenticeships.gov.uk/employers/training-your-apprentice (accessed 16 December 2022).

HM Revenue and Customs (HMRC) (2016) Pay Apprenticeship Levy Guidance. [online] Available at: www.gov.uk/guidance/pay-apprenticeship-levy (accessed 16 December 2022).

Home Office (2019) National Campaign to Recruit 20,000 Police Officers Launches Today. [online] Available at: www.gov.uk/government/news/national-campaign-to-recruit-20000-police-officers-launches-today (accessed 16 December 2022).

Institute for Apprenticeships and Technical Education (IfATE) (2017) *End Point Assessment Plan for Police Constable Integrated Degree Apprenticeship at Level 6*. [online] Available at: www.instituteforapprenticeships.org/media/1440/police-constable-assessment-plan.pdf (accessed 16 December 2022).

Institute for Apprenticeships and Technical Education (IfATE) (2018) *Police Constable (Integrated Degree)*. [online] Available at: www.instituteforapprenticeships.org/apprenticeship-standards/police-constable-integrated-degree-v1-0 (accessed 16 December 2022).

Kolb, D A (1984) *Experiential Learning: Experience as a Source of Learning and Development*. Upper Saddle River, NJ: Prentice Hall.

Moon, J (1999) *Reflection in Learning and Professional Development*. Oxford: Routledge Falmer.

National Police Chiefs' Council (NPCC) (2016) *Policing Vision 2025*. [online] Available at: www.npcc.police.uk/documents/Policing%20Vision.pdf (accessed 16 December 2022).

Police (Conduct) Regulations 2008. [online] Available at: www.legislation.gov.uk/uksi/2008/2864/contents/made (accessed 16 December 2022).

Sparkes, V (2014) *RAISE Model for Policing Practitioners*. Sheffield: Sheffield Hallam University.

University of Greenwich (2022) Learning and Teaching: Formative v Summative. [online] Available at: www.gre.ac.uk/learning-teaching/assessment/assessment/design/formative-vs-summative (accessed 16 December 2022).

Appendix 1 Mapping of the Police Constable Apprenticeship Standards to the EPA (KSBs)

Knowledge: the police constable will know and understand	How is it assessed?	By whom?
The ethics and values of professional policing, including duty of care, service delivery, employment practice, efficiency, effectiveness and value for money, Code of Ethics, professional standards, equality, diversity and human rights **(K1)**.	Professional discussion	Independent Assessor
Key cross-cutting and inter-dependent areas of policing, including: roles and responsibilities, criminal justice, counter terrorism, vulnerability (including public protection and mental health) and risk **(K2)**.	Professional discussion	Independent Assessor
Applicable aspects of Authorised Professional Practice (APP) (the official source of policing professional practice www.app.college.police.uk) legal and organisational requirements relating to the operational policing context (response, community, intelligence, investigation and roads/transport), including how to: • effectively respond to incidents, preserving scenes and evidence when necessary; • manage and resolve conflict safely and lawfully; • arrest, detain and report individuals safely and lawfully; • conduct diligent and efficient, priority and high-volume investigations; • effectively interview victims, witnesses and suspects; • systematically gather, submit and share information and intelligence to further policing-related outcomes; • meticulously and ethically search individuals, vehicles, premises and outside and virtual spaces; • optimise the use of available technology; • risk manage health and safety for others **(K3)**.	Professional discussion	Independent Assessor

How to interpret and apply the letter and essence of all relevant law, as it relates to any encountered policing situation, incident or context **(K4)**.	Professional discussion	Independent Assessor
Social behaviour and society, including their origins, development, organisation, networks and institutions and how this relates to policing across diverse and increasingly complex communities **(K5)**.	Evidence-based research project	Independent Assessor
The causes, mitigations and prevention of crime and how this knowledge and understanding can influence and be applied to accountable decision-making in all operational policing environments **(K6)**.	Evidence-based research project	Independent Assessor
In-depth knowledge, understanding and expertise relevant to organisational/local needs, including the following operational policing contexts: response, community, intelligence, investigation and roads/transport **(K7)**.	Evidence-based research project	Independent Assessor
Different approaches to systematic evidence-based preventative policing, including how to critically analyse, interpret, implement, share and evaluate findings to problem solve and further positive outcomes. These may relate to internal organisational practice or external social or criminal factors **(K8)**.	Evidence-based research project	Independent Assessor

Skills: the police constable will safely and lawfully be able to	How is it assessed?	By whom?
Apply Authorised Professional Practice (www.app.college.police.uk) and any local policy applicable to the operational policing context **(S1)**.	Professional discussion	Independent Assessor
Communicate effectively, in accordance with the varied needs of differing situations, individuals, groups and communities. Use own communication skills to manage planned and uncertain situations, and to persuade/lead others as needed **(S2)**.	Professional discussion	Independent Assessor
Gather, handle and accurately analyse information and intelligence from a variety of sources to support law enforcement and to maximise policing effectiveness **(S3)**.	Professional discussion (core skills and knowledge)/EBRP (specialist skills and knowledge)	Independent Assessor
Manage dynamic conflict situations in policing through leadership, and by dealing with a wide range of behaviours and incidents, taking personal accountability for the use of proportionate and justifiable responses and actions **(S4)**.	Professional discussion	Independent Assessor
Manage effective and ethical searches for evidence and information in differing environments. Take responsibility for courses of action required to follow up on findings (within remit of own role) to maintain the peace and uphold the law **(S5)**.	Professional discussion	Independent Assessor

Skills: the police constable will safely and lawfully be able to	How is it assessed?	By whom?
Provide an initial, autonomous and ongoing response to incidents, which can be complex, confrontational and life threatening, to bring about the best possible outcomes. Provide an initial, autonomous response to crime scenes, where encountered, that require the management and preservation of evidence and exhibits **(S6)**.	Professional discussion	Independent Assessor
Provide leadership to protect the public, and empathetic and appropriate support to victims, witnesses and vulnerable people **(S7)**.	Professional discussion	Independent Assessor
Manage and conduct effective and efficient priority and high-volume investigations. Use initiative to diligently progress investigations, identifying, evaluating and following lines of enquiry to inform the possible initiation of criminal proceedings. Apply an investigative mind-set when decision-making. Present permissible evidence to authorities where required **(S8)**.	Professional discussion/EBRP	Independent Assessor
Interview victims, witnesses and suspects (including those who may be non-compliant, or have been intimidated or coerced) effectively, in relation to a range of investigations, some of which may be multi-dimensional **(S9)**.	Professional discussion/EBRP	Independent Assessor
Assess risk and threats across increasingly complex policing contexts, to take decisions and evaluate initiatives and their outcomes, including the impact of differing actions and methods, in accordance with the policing national decision-making model and evidence-based principles. Take account of best available evidence from a wide array of sources, including research and analysis, when making decisions. Apply justified discretion when appropriate and it is in the public interest to do so **(S10)**.	Professional discussion EBRP	Independent Assessor
Use police powers to deal with suspects, victims and witnesses across various challenging situations, conducting all actions in a balanced, proportionate and justifiable manner **(S11)**.	Professional discussion	Independent Assessor
Proactively introduce new ways of working and innovation to police work where appropriate and possible and apply critical thinking across policing activities within own area of responsibility **(S12)**.	Presentation plus panel discussion	Independent Assessor led, supported by employer and lead-HEI
Plan, apply and evaluate different policing approaches alongside partner organisations or as part of a multi-disciplinary team to address identified, often complex, issues, concerns and situations to reduce and prevent crime in communities. Provide supportive leadership to community groups, making informed decisions that encourage the delivery of localised strategies **(S13)**.	Presentation plus panel discussion	Independent Assessor led, supported by employer and lead-HEI

Behaviours	What is required?	How is it assessed?	By whom?
Taking accountability (**B1**).	Being accountable and taking ownership for own role and responsibilities, whilst being effective and willing to take appropriate, justifiable risks.	Professional discussion Presentation plus panel only if further confirmation is required	Independent Assessor Independent Assessor led, supported by employer and lead-HEI
Professional integrity (**B2**).	Maintain the highest standards of professionalism and trustworthiness, making sure that values, moral codes and ethical standards are always upheld, including challenging others where appropriate.	Professional discussion EBRP Presentation plus panel discussion only if further confirmation is required	Independent Assessor Independent Assessor led, supported by employer and lead-HEI
Emotionally astute (**B3**).	Understand and effectively manage own emotions in stressful situations, understanding motivations and underlying reasons for own behaviour and that of others, including colleagues. Value diversity and difference in approaches to work, thinking and background. Treat people with sensitivity, compassion and warmth.	Professional discussion Presentation plus panel discussion only if further confirmation is required	Independent Assessor Independent Assessor led, supported by employer and lead-HEI
Curious and innovative (**B4**).	Have an inquisitive and outward-looking nature, searching for new information to understand alternative sources of best practice and implement creative working methods. Committed to reflecting on how own role is undertaken, learning from success and mistakes to continuously review and adapt approach.	Professional discussion Presentation plus panel discussion only if further confirmation is required	Independent Assessor Independent Assessor led, supported by employer and lead-HEI

Collaborative **(B5)**.	Working effectively with colleagues and external partners, sharing skills, knowledge and insights as appropriate to lead to the best possible results.	Professional discussion Presentation plus panel discussion only if further confirmation is required	Independent Assessor Independent Assessor led, supported by employer and lead-HEI
Supportive and inspirational leading **(B6)**.	Role model the police service's values in day-to-day activities, providing inspiration and clarity to colleagues and stakeholders. Consider how the wider organisation and others are impacted and help others to deliver their objectives effectively.	Professional discussion Presentation plus panel discussion only if further confirmation is required	Independent Assessor Independent Assessor led, supported by employer and lead-HEI

(IfATE, 2017, p 17)

Reference

Institute for Apprenticeships and Technical Education (2017) Police Constable Assessment Plan. [online] Available at: www.instituteforapprenticeships.org/media/1440/police-constable-assessment-plan.pdf (accessed 12 December 2022).

Appendix 2 Professional discussion: assessment criteria underpinning KSBs/operational competence

A professional discussion (following a review of the Operational Competence Portfolio [OCP] by the Independent Assessor) assesses the application of all core workplace-based policing KSBs, ie operational competence. A consistent national approach is critical within policing to ensure inter-operability and high-quality outcomes for stakeholders including the public. This is achieved by:

- the grading of the professional discussion utilising the 13 assessment criteria that underpin the KSBs, which in turn map to the OCP collated pre-gateway;
- the format and content of the OCP forming part of a Police Constable Degree Apprenticeship specification within the National Policing Curriculum (NPC), which is maintained by the professional body (the College of Policing).

The assessment and subsequent grading of the professional discussion must consider whether the apprentice has met the following 13 distinct areas of operational competence.

Assessment criteria I	Candidates will be able to demonstrate the following to evidence competence
Operating in accordance with the law, authorised professional practice and the Code of Ethics	In the operational policing workplace, demonstrate knowledge and understanding of the legal and professional practice requirements relating to the professional policing activities set out in II to IX below (this assessment document) having due regard to the Code of Ethics and the National Decision Model (NDM).

→

Assessment criteria II	Candidates will be able to demonstrate the following to evidence competence
Providing an initial response to policing incidents	Provide an initial response to incidents in line with legal and professional practice requirements including: • using the THRIVE approach; • communicating effectively with those at the scene; • controlling incidents, preserving the scene and potential evidence; • recognising and providing support to vulnerable individuals (including casualties); • providing support to victims and witnesses of the incident; • engaging in appropriate multi-agency referrals; • recording actions taken.

Assessment criteria III	Candidates will be able to demonstrate the following to evidence competence
Managing conflict in a professional policing context	Apply conflict management and personal safety techniques with issued equipment, including: • making threat assessments using all available information; • using approved and appropriate communication techniques; • recognising danger cues; • applying appropriate and proportionate tactical options and conflict management techniques; • recording all actions taken and decisions made in line with legal and organisational procedures.

Assessment criteria IV	Candidates will be able to demonstrate the following to evidence competence
Providing support to vulnerable people, victims and witnesses	• Communicate effectively with vulnerable people, victims and witnesses. • Provide appropriate support to vulnerable people, victims and witnesses. • Demonstrate an understanding of the factors pertaining to vulnerable individuals, victims and witnesses that may influence their ability and willingness to receive support. • Assess the resilience and capability of the individual, and provide further support (including referrals) as appropriate.

Assessment criteria V	Candidates will be able to demonstrate the following to evidence competence
Using police powers to deal with suspects	• Arrest and detain suspects in line with legal and organisational requirements and timescales. • Report suspects in line with legal and organisational requirements and timescales. • Apply alternative options with regard to disposal of suspects, in line with organisational requirements.

Assessment criteria VI	Candidates will be able to demonstrate the following to evidence competence
Conducting police searches	Conduct safe, lawful and effective police searches of premises, vehicles and outside spaces including: • communicating appropriately with those at the search scene; • identifying the correct search areas; • protecting search scenes; • preventing loss or contamination of potential evidence; • utilising approved search techniques; • analysing the significance of items found during the search; • seizing items covered by identified search powers; • maintaining the integrity of seized items; • leaving the search scene in the required condition; • documenting all decisions, actions, options and rationales.

Assessment criteria VII	Candidates will be able to demonstrate the following to evidence competence
Conducting police searches of individuals	Conduct police searches of individuals in line with legal and organisational requirements including: • using authorised and appropriate systematic search methods; • communicating appropriately with the individual before and during the search; • controlling individuals in order to prevent loss or contamination of evidence, escape of individual(s) and/or harm to any person; • maintaining personal safety using approved and appropriate techniques; • seizing any identified items covered by the relevant search power; • maintaining the integrity of seized items; • informing individuals being searched of the results of the search and any further actions to be taken; • documenting all decisions, actions, options and rationale.

Assessment criteria VIII	Candidates will be able to demonstrate the following to evidence competence
Conducting priority and volume investigations	Conduct priority and volume investigations including: • planning and conducting an initial investigation; • gathering information, intelligence and evidence to support investigation; • undertaking investigative and evidential evaluation throughout the investigation; • briefing relevant others regarding the progress of the investigation; • identifying the need for any other additional support, including escalation; • identifying and working with victims, potential witnesses and suspects; • dealing with suspects in line with investigative decision-making; • providing victims, witnesses and their families with information, support and protection in accordance with their needs; • retain and record the details of an investigation.

Assessment criteria IX	Candidates will be able to demonstrate the following to evidence competence
Interviewing victims, witnesses and suspects	Plan and prepare interviews with victims, witnesses and suspects. Conduct interviews with victims, witnesses and suspects including: • explaining the interview process to those present and confirming understanding; • maintaining the security and welfare of those present; • using approved interview and communication techniques to obtain accurate accounts; • using exhibits in line with approved interview techniques; • addressing any contingencies that may arise during the interview; • completing all necessary documents and records; • closing the interview, informing all present of the next steps. And, for suspect interviews: • delivering pre-interview briefings to legal representatives; • using the required cautions, evidential or special warnings and checking suspect's understanding; • evaluate interviews with victims, witnesses and suspects and carry out post-interview procedures.

Assessment criteria X	Candidates will be able to demonstrate the following to evidence competence
Response policing	Provide an effective initial response to a critical incident

Assessment criteria XI	Candidates will be able to demonstrate the following to evidence competence
Policing communities	• Communicate and engage proactively with communities, including through use of social media. • Foster productive partnerships in community policing.

Assessment criteria XII	Candidates will be able to demonstrate the following to evidence competence
Information and intelligence	• Conduct effective analysis and evaluation of information and intelligence. • Develop information and intelligence to inform the tasking and co-ordination process.

Assessment criteria XIII	Candidates will be able to demonstrate the following to evidence competence
Conducting investigations	• Demonstrate appropriate strategies for dealing with more complex police interviews. • Apply appropriate investigative procedures in respect of internet-facilitated crime.

(IfATE, 2017, p 22)

Reference

Institute for Apprenticeships and Technical Education (IfATE) (2017) *End Point Assessment Plan for Police Constable Integrated Degree Apprenticeship at Level 6.* [online] Available at: www.instituteforapprenticeships.org/media/1440/police-constable-assessment-plan.pdf (accessed 16 December 2022).

Index

Page numbers in **bold** refer to tables and in *italic* refer to figures.

accountability, 5
additional learning needs (ALNs), 32
advice and support, finding, 40
Apprenticeship Levy, 7
assessments. *See also* end-point assessment (EPA)
   guidelines and requirements, 98
   location for, 84
   logging on early for, 84
   methods, 20–1
   overview, 20
   planning, 44
at risk people, support to, 17
attention deficit disorder (ADD), 32
attention deficit (hyperactivity) disorder (ADHD), 32
autism spectrum condition (ASC), 32
autonomy, 5, 17
awarding the EPA, 104–5

behaviours, and PC apprenticeship standards, 119–20
benefits of apprenticeship, 30
best available evidence, 53
body-worn cameras (BWC), 16

case studies, 26–7, 46, 64–5, 79, 102–4
coaching, 69–70
   considerations when planning/participating in, 71
   definition of, 69–70
Code of Ethics, 13, 85, 86, 121
College of Policing (CoP), 5, 7, 13
communication and engagement skills, 17
communities, policing, 17, 18, 24, 94, 124
competencies element, 31
Competency and Values Framework, 13
complex police interviews, 95–6
conducting investigations, 18, 24, 26, 124
confidence level, 69
conflict management skills, 17, 69, 87–8, 122
criminal justice system, 18
criticality/critical thinking, 17, 60–2
   analysis stage, 63
   application stage, 63
   assignment recap, **64**
   comprehension stage, 62–3
   evaluation stage, 63
   knowledge stage, 62
   synthesis stage, 63
   in writing, **62**
curriculum, 5, 11, 12, 15–16
   comprehensive range of policing professional situations and contexts, 16–17
   effective performance in key, specific areas of professional policing responsibility, 17–18
   professional performance in core areas of policing, 18

data collection limitations, 57–8
data scrutiny, 58
decision-making, 17
Degree Holder Entry Programme (DHEP), 9, 10
   key aspects of, 9
   qualification for, 9
Degree in Professional Police Practice, 12
descriptive writing and critical writing, differences between, **62**
digital policing, 17
diversity, 16
drinking water during assessment, 83
dyscalculia, 32
dysgraphia, 32
dyslexia, 32
dyspraxia, 32

EBRP. *See* evidence-based research project (EBRP)
Education and Skills Funding Agency, 35
end point assessment (EPA), 12, 26. *See also* assessments
   assessment components, 69
   assessment structure, 82–3
   awarding, 104–5
   grading information for, **105**
   and Independent Assessors, 66–7
   and police force representative, 67
   preparing for, 83–4
   professional discussion. *See* professional discussion
   resits and retakes of, 52–3
   standardisation of, 80
   and university representative, 67

Index • 127

equality, 16
Equality Act 2010, 31, 32
equality of opportunity, 31–3
essays, 43
essential study skills, 40
ethics
    in EBRP, 58–9
    in policing, 13, 16
evidence-based policing, 16, 18
evidence-based research project (EBRP), 9, 53, 97
    academic support and supervision, 54–5
    assessment criteria, 59
    checklist, 111
    data collection limitations, 57–8
    data scrutiny, 58
    ethical considerations and standards, 58–9
    grading, **60**
    literature review, 56
    methodology considerations, 57
    overview of, 54
    research data and statistics, 58
    staff expectations, 55
    starting of, 56
    student expectations, 55
    teaching method, 54
    types of, 56–7
examination
    planning, 44
    preparation, 44
expectations of PCDA programme, 30–1
experiential learning, 72
    abstract conceptualisation, 73
    active experimentation, 73
    concrete experience, 73
    reflective observation, 73

face-to-face delivery, 20
final submission, checking and proofreading, 42–3
first impressions, 83
Force Occupational Competencies (FOC), 80
formative assessment, 72
formatting, 43
front-line policing, 18
Full Operational Competence (FOC), 21, 25, 70

gateway, 52, 68
grading information, **105**
graduation, 50–23

human rights, 16

Independent Assessors (IAs), 66–7, 81–2
    tips for preparing for EPA, 83–4
Independent Patrol Status (IPS), 10, 21, 50–23
information and intelligence, 18, 24, 95, 124
initial planning of an investigation, 91–2
Initial Police Learning and Development Programme (IPLDP), 6, 13

Institute for Apprenticeships and Technical Education (IfATE) 15
Intelligence Support Officer (ISO), 26
interviews, investigative, 92–3, 95–6, 124

key skills element, 31
knowledge, and PC apprenticeship standards, 116
knowledge, skills, and behaviours (KSBs), 11, 15, 34, 35, 52, 84, 116–20

leadership skills, 17
learning as a cycle, 74
learning blocks, 19, 20
legal and professional responsibilities, understanding, 16
location for assessment, 84
logging on early for assessment, 84

mentoring, 69
    considerations when planning/participating in, 71
    definition of, 70
milestones, 106
    final EPA day, 109–12
    professional discussion element of EPA, preparing for, 50
    Year 1, 107
    Year 1 level 4, 49–50
    Year 1 review, 51
    Year 2, 107–8
    Year 2 review, 51
    Year 3, 108–9
    Year 3 level 6, 52
minimum requirements, in apprentice standards, 52
mock EPA, 77, 83
    activities, 77
    expectations from, 77–8
    post session, 78–9
    tips for, 77

national apprenticeship standard, 14–15
National Decision Model (NDM), 85, 85–6
National Investigators Exam (NIE), 10, 26
National Police Chiefs' Council (NPCC), 4, 5, 10
national policing curriculum. See curriculum

off-the-job training, 35–8
Operational Competence Portfolio (OCP), 21, 26, 49, 68, 84

panel discussion, 98, 100
    checklist, 111
    literature review, 100–1
    questions regarding presentation, 100–1
    tips for, 98–9
partnership working skills, 17
PC apprenticeship standards, 116–20
perplexity, 75
personal safety, 122

personal safety techniques, 87–8
police
  role as your employer, 34
  support from, 22
Police Constable Degree Apprenticeship (PCDA), 7
  and Apprenticeship Levy, 7
  benefits of, 7–8
  key aspects of, 8–9
  qualification for, 8
Police Constable Degree Apprenticeship programme, 12–13
police force representative, for EPA, 67
police powers to deal with suspects, 88–9, 122
police recruitment and training, recommendations for, 5
police recruitment pathways, changes to, 4–5
policing communities, 17, 18, 24, 94, 124
Policing Education Qualifications Framework (PEQF)
  aims of, 7
  collaborative approach to education, 14
  and continuing professional development, 14
  educational principles of, 13–14
  ensuing national consistency of professional education, 13
  entry routes, 11, 28
  equality of educational opportunity, 13–14
  high-quality, evidence-based education, 14
  meeting the professional requirements, 13
  overview, 5–6
  programmes, 7–10
  values-based, ethical approach to policing, 13
policing strategies, 16
policing the roads, 18, 24
Policing Vision 2025, 3, 4–5, 10
portfolio, 50–1, 83
preparing for EPA, 83–4
presentation, 98, 99–100
  assessment guidance for, **102**
  checklist, 111
  layout, 100–1
  tips for, 98–9
primary data, 56
priority and volume investigations, 123
professional development, 22–3
  advanced, 25–6
  continuing, 24–5
  and graduation, 50–23
  initial, 23–4
professional discretion, 17
professional discussion (PD), 84, 121–4
  checklist, 110
  grading, **96–7**
  questions and examples, 85–96
  tips for, 84–5
Professional Policing Degree (PPD), 9
  key aspects of, 10
  qualification for, 10

professional resilience, 17
Professionalising Investigation Programme (PIP) accreditations, 10, 26
public protection, 17

RAISE model of reflection, 76
reflection
  definition of, 74–5
  RAISE model of, 76
reflective practice, 72
  experiential learning. See experiential learning
  learing as a cycle, 74
  utilisation of, 75–6
research project, 26
research skills, 16
resits and retakes
  guidance checklist, 112
  overview, 52–3
response policing, 18, 24, 93–4, 124

searches, 123
  of an individual, 90–1, 123
  lawful and effective, 89–90
secondary data, 56
self-directed distance learning, 20
self-reflection, 17, 96
skills, and PC apprenticeship standards, 117
SMART coaching and mentoring, 38–40
social interaction, 69
social media, 16
standardisation
  definition of, 79–80
  of the EPA, 80
start of assessment, checklist, 110
starting the apprenticeship
  day one, 19–20
  overview, 18–19
study and academic skills
  preparing work for submission, 41
  writing essentials, 41
submissions
  date and time of, 45
  guidance for, 43
summative assessment, 72
support and learning triangle, *30*
supporting vulnerable people, victims and witnesses, 17, 88, 122
suspects
  interviews with, 92–3, 124
  police powers to deal with, 88–9, 122

team working skills, 17
technical knowledge element, 31
terrorism, counteracting, 17
THRIVE approach, 86–7, 122
tripartite meetings, 33–5, **36**, **38**
tutor constables, 70–1

university
  programme, 20
  representative, 67
  support at, 22

victims and witnesses
  interviews with, 92–3, 124
  support to, 88, 122
virtual online environment (VLE), 21, 45, 54, 58
vulnerable people, support to, 17, 88

well-being management, 17
What Works Centre, 9
witnesses. *See* victims and witnesses
word-count requirements, 42
work-based assessment within policing, 72
work-based coach, role of, 34
work-based OCP, 68
work–life balance, 45–6
workplace-based policing, 84
writing essentials, 41
written reports, 43